**Observations of a Straight White
Male with No Interesting Fetishes**

OBSERVATIONS OF A STRAIGHT WHITE
MALE WITH NO INTERESTING FETISHES

Observations of a Straight White
Male with No Interesting Fetishes

Printed in the United States of America

ISBN: 978-0-9853181-4-7

12by3 Press
P.O. Box 110126
263 S 4th St.
Brooklyn, NY 11211-9997

www.12by3.com

For Ria

Full Disclosure: OCD 1

UMass 5

The Mating Habits of the Knobelsdorf 21

Jose Armando Vasquez Lopez 32

Excuse Me, Sorry, Thank You 37

Dating 101: Rotation 40

Acceptable Losses 45

Men Going Their Own Way 54

Full Disclosure: Rage 66

Someone Bless Our Weird Fucking Country 70

The View from up Here 80

Formative Moments 86

Dating 101: Comedy 110

Online Dating 115

Dating Advice for the End of Civilization 128

Full Disclosure: Anxiety 134

Prudent iSex 139

What Is and What Should Never Be 143

Sabbath and Coral 150

Notches 161

Nobody's Bitch 169

Dating 101: Median 180

Italy, 1996 183

24 Hours of Privilege 195

For Fuck's Sake, Irene 207

Inadequate Reminders 216

Eulogy 222

Full Disclosure: Dealing 238

Observations of a Straight White Male with No Interesting
Fetishes 241

Dating 101: The Right Amount of Sky 253

FULL DISCLOSURE: OCD

I have an awkward relationship with rationality. For instance, I can spend a good twenty minutes talking about new-age spiritualist magic.[*] The practitioners seem compelled to imbue every goddamn thing they see with a spirit, unless it's been run through a machine because machines apparently extract spirits from base elements, so a lump of iron on the ground somehow has more soul than a Toyota.[†] Auras are a glitch in color differential processing in your brain; you see them for the same reason you see hallucinatory dots in grid patterns. Any photographs of auras are similar glitches in the photographic (or, lately, Photoshopic) process. Plants do not speak or have long-term goals or feelings as we know them. The hills are not alive, no matter how many troublesome nuns decide to sing on them. There is no Earth spirit, and you can't arrange rocks to get better luck.

---

[*] And no, adding a *k* to the end does not lift sleight of hand into the realm of "True Magick."

[†] Although Volkswagen seems to have a manufacturing process that prevents this.

After these twenty minutes are over, the timer will go off on my oven, and if perchance a single piece of Mueller's pasta falls out of the strainer, my anxiety about food contamination will prevent me from just rinsing it off and tossing it back in, while my babbling crazy forces me to toss a few more pieces after it so it won't be lonely.

You read that right.

I throw away food to prevent already thrown-out food from being lonely.

I even tell little stories in my head of the adventures they'll have: the fallings-out, their desperate attempts to hide from the rats seeking their succulent starchy goodness soaked in trash juice, whispering, "Don't move, their vision's based on motion," the romantic triangles, oh God, there are three in there now, what if two go off together and leave the third one alone, whoops that was two more and now there's the same problem unless they're Mormon but of course they aren't, why would pasta be Mormon?

In my attempts to make sure there's an even number of escapees, or at least enough so that I can't tell how many there are and can stop worrying about their relationship problems, I toss out enough pasta to provide a healthy genetic pool for future generations.

Considering I cooked pasta almost every day for ten years, and still make it three or four times a week, I've probably thrown out a hundred pounds of food via this method. At no point has the rational part of my brain that I'm so proud of said, "What the fuck are you doing? For God's sake, STOP

THROWING FOOD AWAY. IT'S NOT LONELY. IT WAS DEAD
WHEAT SIX MONTHS BEFORE YOU DROPPED IT IN BOILING
WATER." Also, it has only crossed my mind in the most academic sense that the pasta that didn't escape spends the rest of
its brief existence doused in hot, acidic tomato sauce before
being ground apart by my teeth, swallowed, and slowly disin-
tegrated into its component nutrients. Then, whatever remains, I flush down a toilet. I also have no issues with the
tomatoes, the carcasses of which I prefer to tear apart with my
bare hands before salting them and slowly bringing them to
boil. The fact that the tomatoes come out of a can in tomato
juice and have slightly less individuality means they could
never have feelings like my poor—but never lonely—pasta
fugitives. Perhaps most disturbing, the private life of spaghetti
is easier on my nerves. Because I'm aware my OCD won't let
me stop this, I try to take a rational stance on needing to satisfy an irrational need: to avoid wasting more spaghetti after a
strand escapes, I break it into as many pieces as needed, confident that I did not dismember one healthy individual but
instead created a dozen smaller ones, like any psychotic and
omnipotent being should.

And if my ethical stance on discarded food is so stringent
that I need to ensure they have communities large enough to
survive hereditary blood diseases, I should probably reexamine
my stance on the food I actually consume, or even think
harder about the food I eat that once made noise and moved
around. Do I? No.

This habitual food sacrifice evolved from having stuffed animals and watching Disney specials as a kid. As a kid, anything can have any quality you want. Of course the stuffed animals feel bad, or the car is angry, or the sky is bored. Before our hard-won human legacy of science kicks in, natural causality doesn't really make sense, so we assume the budding thoughts in our own heads are what cause everything else. I would make loud noise if I was really angry, so the black cloud over my head clearly just walked in on its sister knocking over its Lego castle. My stuffed animals are all neatly arranged somewhere, where they can all see and breathe, so they can live out an eternity of pointless boredom staring at the walls or one another. My obsession with keeping everybody happy snakes deep into emotionally unbalanced territory whenever practical concerns don't figure into the situation enough to trigger practical logic. What I call rational thinking is the successful application of some breathtakingly broken tools to get through the day without too much anxiety. I have about an 80 percent success rate.

Due to substance-abuse habits at the time, this is approximately everything I remember about going to UMass Amherst.

Shortly after I arrived, some jackasses flew planes into the World Trade Center. I discovered this after staying awake all night watching Fellini movies and snorting Adderall, and exactly two minutes before I walked into the student union on September 11, 2001, I was concocting a satirical short film in my head. The script centered around two CEOs and their minions, one set standing on top of the school library and one on top of the union. They were each devising ways to blow up the other building for nonsense reasons. I showed up in front of the cafeteria TV just in time to see the second plane hit, and my first thought was, *This is my fault.*

It wasn't, of course. I freaked out anyway because most of my friends were in the city for various reasons, and there was no cell phone service at that point. I went back to my dorm and wandered around in a daze, ending up in a stranger's room where there was a TV. I don't remember what network was on, but it played a clip of smiling children and people celebrating, and the newscaster said something like, "Here they are celebrating in [middle-eastern nation] upon hearing news of the towers falling." I later discovered that the clip they played was from the early nineties and the people in it were celebrating a holiday. It had nothing to do with us. Somehow, this got swept under the rug over the next few months, but it did its job in the confusion of the moment.

My RA swept past me. She was useless at the best of times; that day she just kept repeating, "I can't deal with this," stuffed a few clothes in a bag, and found a bus back to Wisconsin.

Later that night, I went to town to pick up some booze and passed another RA from my building.

"Hey Pete. Where are you headed?"

"Picking up beer."

She laughed at this. "We're having a prayer in the chapel. Do you want to join us?"

"No, that's okay. Atheist."

"What?"

"I'm an atheist."

"What do you mean? You're not Christian?"

"I don't believe in God."

"What do you believe in?"

"Nothing."

"What do you mean?"

I cross myself and offer a kiss to the heavens every time I remember that, between Brooklyn and Google, I don't have to have this conversation anymore. I wrapped it up the way you had to back in those days, mumbling something about it being complicated and changing the subject, then headed to the store, picked up four cans of Guinness, and started back, happily anticipating a brain-silencing buzz. It was about a half-hour walk each way, so the timing worked out just right to catch her coming out of her prayer meeting.

"How was it?"

"It was good! What did you buy?"

I blinked. "Beer. I told you on my way out."

She laughed again. "No, really, what did you get?"

I remembered at this point she was only nineteen, and wasn't used to people just being able to buy beer.

"I really did get beer."

"But you're not twenty-one."

"Yes, I am."

"But you can't drink that in the dorm."

"Yes, I can."

I still wonder what RA training actually consisted of.

"Oh. Well. I guess that's true. But why are you drinking?"

The answer to this question seemed obvious back then and gets more obvious every year, but I made some effort:

"Two giant fucking buildings just collapsed because planes flew into them. If there was ever an excuse to drink, I think I've got one."

"You shouldn't drink to solve your problems."

To be fair, she turned out to be right.

◆

Over the next few days of artificial trauma-bonding, I started developing a crush on one of my neighbors, and in my innocent young mind things were going well until, three weeks into our friendship and midway through a conversation, I looked down and realized she had no right hand.

The thought that slapped me in the brain and silenced my contributions to the conversation was, *How the hell did I not notice that?* followed by, *Did that happen recently?* but that couldn't have been true since she probably would have been out of school for a few days if she'd lost it since I last talked to her.

From her perspective, I just stopped talking and stared at her wrist stump, and I doubt she interpreted the horror on my face as being directed at my own obliviousness, and the remainder of our relationship had an awkward feel to it. I later asked her for her AIM screen name in—and I knew this even as I heard the awful noises tremble through my vocal cords—the most cinematically stalker-creepy way a twenty-one-year-old college student could muster. Naturally, I engaged in an early form of e-stalking and found her LiveJournal, which had a line something like this: "I expect my creepy neighbor is sipping his coffee and reading this right now."

I looked down at my coffee, said, "Goddammit," turned off my computer, and went to find weed.

◆

Smoking weed and sipping whiskey with Jun in Northampton was the capstone for every attempt I made at a romantic relationship that year, sort of like a repetitive sitcom where the protagonist always learns a lesson but never actually grows. As Marty unto Frasier, as Wilson unto Tim, so Jun unto to me, and for exactly the same amount of good.

Since the last bus back to Amherst usually left twenty minutes before I was done getting stoned, I often found myself on Jun's couch or in need of a cab. One night in winter, I accidentally called a limo.

Just as I was getting over my surprise at the car I ordered being twice the length I expected, a gene-splicing experiment between a Blue Meanie and Les Claypool popped out of the driver's side. It was dressed in a two-tone leather tuxedo covered in skulls, chains, and checker patterns, and accented by a top hat. It smiled broadly, ran around the car and opened the back door.

"Hop in, sir!"

If I must die, I'd prefer to die strangely, and this seemed as good a time as any, so I got in.

The Les Meanie spent the next thirty minutes talking about being a biker back in the day and how many people get shot around Holyoke. I tried to contribute to the conversation until he asked me if I liked Southern rock. I figured I knew the words to "Sweet Home Alabama," so I said sure and spent the rest of the ride listening to songs about how much fun it is to round up the boys and hang niggers. I let him talk at me as I gaped at the speakers and clutched the door handle, wishing I could sober up.

◆

I met a girl on a bus right before spring break. She had an unusual name, which she said meant something like "prayer" or "brotherhood." I don't remember, I just remember saying, "Lucky it didn't mean frog burp." Despite this, she gave me her phone number.

I called her two weeks after the local cluster of colleges got back from break. I opened with the usual shy guy, "I don't know if you remember me, but—" and she cut me off with, "Oh my God, I'd almost given up."

I was in.

I don't remember the date we had, I just remember us making out in her Spartan dorm room with fifteen-foot ceilings. She was tall and smart and said her previous boyfriend, whom her parents wanted her to marry, took her for granted. That was not going to be a problem for me, but I was savvy enough at this point not to be creepy about it.

We made a date for Valentine's Day, and she stood me up. I wandered around Northampton waiting for some kind of contact, giving up around nine. I thought, *Fuck it,* and went to see *Amélie,* which had just opened.

I walked out feeling as good as I'd ever felt in my life. My review of *Amélie* is this: You can be stood up by your dream girl on February 14th, watch this movie, and go to bed happy.

She went back to her ex. I like to assume he's taking her for granted.

◆

The Captain sat down next to my friend and me in a pizza joint and began reading aloud something between an insane manifesto and a cutting screed of political journalism, and every single sentence was dripping with sexual innuendo. It was written in what looked like crayon on what looked like home-pulped paper. It might have been the most brilliant writing I'd ever heard, it might have been total psychosis. He wore a hat and shades and was sharply dressed, though he looked like he'd been sharply dressed for several days. A cigarette holder was clenched between his teeth, and nothing would surprise me less than to find out he was Hunter S. Thompson on a bender in the Berkshires, but I don't know what Thompson looked like in 2001, and the memory's too dim to get an accurate comparison anymore. The only name we ever got out of him was The Captain. Maybe he was a Time Lord on acid.

We ran around smoking pot with him until 2:00 a.m., checked out his van full of more bizarre political commentary on papyrus, and parted ways. He later went after my friend with a knife, then vanished for good.

◆

A student in my building died of a heart attack while doing push-ups at four in the morning after taking muscle-building pills. This inspired my RA to hold a men's awareness meeting.

"A what?" I said when she asked me to come.

"This really awful thing happened and I think you should come to this meeting."

She explained the details as I blinked at her and finished my beer. I felt bad for the kid and his family, but I was pretty comfortable in my role in society at the time, since it had only been a little over a year since I unlocked the Not Institutionalized achievement. Still, it was something to do on a Tuesday, and I thought of my RA as a sweet little kitten just discovering the world is as full of inescapable bags and shallow bodies of water as it is pretty ribbons and free food, so I liked to help with her little quests to find out how things worked. She thought it was disgusting to use toilet paper to blow your nose when you ran out of Kleenex, so we had a ways to go.

I roped in two of my friends. We called ourselves the Pisces Crazy Club, because we'd all been in mental hospitals and were all Pisces. We consisted of a Boston street thug, equal parts, "This is, like, the third draft of this poem, I can't find the right word for the second verse," and "I don't think he died after the fight but I never checked"; a wide-eyed kid from Texas diving headfirst into everything he could find in this crazy nondesert he'd suddenly found himself in; and me. We were all polite, quiet, and usually trying to study or relax, although only Texas had a girlfriend, so we were a little high-strung.

The presenter was a personal trainer and, apparently, a men's health lecturer. He was nice. Besides him, there were six or seven girls, us (the PCC), and one other guy. We'll call him Ass.

The presenter said, "Men are encouraged to compete, and tend to try to get alpha status in any group—"

"I don't," said Ass.

"Well, in general, men will almost automatically take any situation and try to prove they're better than the other—"

"Not me," said Ass.

The presenter closed his eyes and took a deep breath, during which I—because I was trying to listen and honestly explore men's issues—restrained myself from lunging across the table between me and Ass and screaming, "YOU'RE DOING IT RIGHT NOW YOU FUCKING TWIT," and beating him to death with a chair. Fortunately, he left a couple of minutes later so the rest of us could get on with it.

"Do you size up other men in the room when you walk in?"

Nods from the PCC.

"Do you think about how you could take them in a fight?"

Nods.

"Do you feel like rage is the only acceptable emotion for you, but you're not supposed to act on it?"

Yup.

"Are you afraid of your own rage?"

Constantly.

At this point the girls are looking around the room in horror.

"I'm a little of scared of you guys right now. I never knew men were like this."

The trainer tries to show the scene in *Fight Club* where the two fighters hug after one of them taps out. He can't find it, but he makes his point: Men bond with other men over competition and violence, because that seems like the only safe emotional place for us.

For the PCC, composed of men who have the standard compliment of rage issues plus documented mental instability, it's a relief to be able to talk about this. We tell the girls we don't want to be angry, but men, especially in college, are all vying for alpha status, and the ones who have it get more mates. We're angry when we lose, we have to be angry to win, and we're angry that we have to play at all. We're angry that we get more respect for being angry. We're angry at people saying, "That's not true, you don't have to be angry," when they're playing the same game but shanking from the shadows. We're all trying to diffuse anger outside and inside, because it's going to get expressed one way or another.

We shake the presenter's hand, reassure the girls we're not rapists or woman-haters, pat one another on the back and head out to . . .

"Man that felt good. Let's get some beer," says Boston.

Something changes as we get in the car. I look at Boston and Texas.

"Let's get. A lot. Of fucking. Beer."

"Fucking right."

We grab a thirty rack right before the liquor store closes, take it to the dingy smoking room in the basement of our dorm hall, and proceed to lose our minds.

At some point while we're wrestling, we knock over the sole wooden chair. As opposed to standing it back up, we decide to tear it apart and howl like monkeys. Since it's the only piece of furniture in the room, we stalk out into the non-smoking basement lounge and grab the first comfortable chairs we see from a table of students studying.

"We're taking these."

The rest of the basement steadily clears out as we continue. There's crying. There's singing. We break more furniture. At some point we get sick of walking up to the bathroom so we just start pissing in one of the coffee-can ashtrays, which almost gets knocked over during one of the beer-can fights.

For about five hours, we turned the smoking room into something between an Irish pub at closing time and a frat party. Finally we decide we're hungry, so we go to rob the vending machine. On our way we ask some kids who just sat down, "Hey, you guys want anything?"

"Uh, no?"

"Sure."

Boston walks up to the vending machine, brings his foot up on the last stride for a test kick, and the entire front of the machine instantly shatters.

"Holy shit!"

"Jesus, I thought I'd at least have to give it a couple of whacks."

"Grab it all!"

The kids we'd just spoken to made a hasty exit. We grabbed everything we could carry and ran back to my room, cackling like five-year-olds.

I woke up the next day in about eighty dollars' worth of junk food to Boston knocking on my door.

"Dude," he said, blinking, "what the fuck happened to us?"

Texas came in a moment later. He looked at the bags of chips, candy bars, and various inedible Hostess snacks on my floor.

"Oh shit, we really did that."

◆

Not having sex for my year at UMass despite being older than everyone around me, more experienced in much of what it's possible to be experienced in, and incredibly horny is the best circumstantial evidence I have for the existence of an angry god.

My particular dorm setup had its disadvantages. My roommate was probably the least appealing person I've ever met. After three months, I hated his laugh, and that marks the absolute end of any chance for a reasonable relationship. He watched TV for twelve-hour stretches, switching channels once every two to five seconds, pausing for whole minutes if he chanced upon an explosion or a bikini. He would occasionally pass out during these marathons and drool over the edge of the bed, when he wasn't snoring in four-part harmony.

At first I felt sorry for him, but my sympathy waned as the endless stream of "Fags are weird," "I don't trust black people," and "Jews will screw you" poured out of his mouth. Occasionally I would force him to watch a whole show, and every time a girl was nice to someone, he would say, "Girls aren't really like that, though. Girls are just mean."

So bringing girls home wasn't an option, since he only got out of bed to go to class, or to see his brother, who would come back with him and proceed to call him a "fat, ugly fuck" for three hours. On reflection, I do feel bad for him, but at the time he was just one of the factors between me and a badly needed conjugal visit.

I don't remember what all the other factors were, but I was doing so well picking up girls around town, and going on so many dates, I knew it couldn't be me. On the other hand, by month eight, it really had to be me, because not one of my many dates deemed me worthy of sex. If you can't get laid as a twenty-one year-old at U-fucking-Mass, neighbor to two all-girl schools, you might as well give up. There was probably a class on the taxonomy of daddy issues in Smith College, and I was somehow unable to bed a project partner who all but offered me a blow job.

I was not going to give up. This is how I ended up dating the only Republican at Hampshire College.

Hampshire College allowed a student to graduate whose thesis was hats made out of roadkill. There was more pot there than I've ever seen, and I've seen a lot of pot. It was easier to get a joint than it was to get a cigarette, since well, you know, cigarettes are, like, bad for you, man. I don't know how this girl passed the entrance interview, or why she tried in the first place. But there she was, in the lobby of the building where I had my weekly film class, and she seemed to think I was cute. She also couldn't work a computer to save her life, and though this was long before I knew anything about computers, my ability to read the directions in her homework got my foot in the door. I think she must have been as starved for intimacy as I was, since my mating dance had at that point devolved into a comedy routine.

I call her mouse girl, not only because I can't remember her name. She was short, with curly hair and ears that stuck out a little bit, but I've seen physically mousier girls.* She was also tense yet quiet, with lots of quick little movements, and kept her hands close to her chest a lot.†

So I began courting mouse girl and things were going well. She actually put up with my roommate. As long as we kept off politics, we were fine, and she didn't actually talk that much, so we just got drunk and made out. She was considerably shyer in bed than I would have liked, so it was slow going, but I was making progress.

Then, near the end of the school year, she asked me if I would keep taking classes at Hampshire next year. This is one of the few moments in my life where I wish I had lied. To be clear, it's one of the few because in other moments I either lied and wished I hadn't, or lied and gotten away with it. What I should have said was, "Yes." What I said was, "I'm on exchange from UMaine. I'll be back there next year." What she said was, "Oh."

She stopped taking my calls for the next three weeks, and then I went back to Maine, chaste and ashamed.

Why do I wish I had lied and broken this poor mouse girl's heart by treating her like a disposable object? Because I was twenty-one years old at U-fucking-Mass for a year and I

---

* The clincher for mousiness is shock-straight hair, fairy-slight build, ears sticking out, and anime-huge eyes. Like Fred from *Angel*.
† And she kept nine pet mice. For God's sake, what would you call her behind her back?

hadn't had sex for that entire year, and that seemed really important at the time, because man stuff or something. So I was
faced with living with this fact or having sex. ONCE. With a
Republican! I mean, who really gives a fuck about a Republican? But no. I told the truth, and despite knowing I was a
godless heathen who would have voted for Clinton had I had
the chance, she wanted something more from me than a two-
month relationship, and because of that I have to spend the
rest of my life knowing that I couldn't get laid at UMass. I
am the anti-Tucker Max.

THE MATING HABITS OF THE KNOBELSDORF

I'm attending the New York Comic Con with several goals. My primary objective is to track the elusive Knobelsdorf in its native environment, and ascertain the veracity of its claims pertaining to its "game." In a related goal, I'm here to examine the critical concentration of geek culture, and see how it's evolved since the last convention I attended, which was twenty years ago. In particular, I aim to analyze the gender ratio, its relative attractiveness, and how this affects the romantic climate. The stereotype is that there are ten males for every female, any female has her choice of sex-starved mates, and all the choices are bad. However, according to legend, a slow trickle of socially competent and desirable participants have joined the fray, and these new desirable males can seek out the desirable females and establish communication, as long as they can keep from slipping on the drool of beta males. The Knobelsdorf claims to be a member of this new breed of Comic Con male, and I aim to prove or disprove it. Also, I want a sonic screwdriver.

1:15 p.m., Harefield Road

I have a notebook, a camera, a pen, one hundred and forty dollars in cash, and a pack of cigarettes. I'm wearing shades. I am also overdressed for the weather, so the heat may be an issue. I'm very late, and hungover.

As I finish my brunch, I realize I've lost the cap to my pen. Should have brought the clicky one.

Brunch is fifteen dollars.

Previously

I didn't investigate the website very carefully, except to get directions. There are a lot of pictures of semifamous people and some interior maps which I don't look at, mostly because I see the word *outragity* in large, bold letters on one page and give up. It makes me question my own phrasemashing tendencies, and the line between irony and idiocy. The confirmation e-mail sports jokes I would have found hilarious sixteen years ago: "Don't try to get tricky. We have ninjas and robots waiting to respond at a moment's notice. Our staff of superheroes can verify the legitimate buyer by checking photo ID." I crook exactly one third of my mouth in a way that suggests I understand they were trying to be funny.

1:45 p.m., M Train

I once wanted to hold a game convention, a close cousin of the comic con, in my adopted hometown of Hancock, Maine. My parents vetoed the effort. It was a difficult moment for them, as they were trying to instill liberal, egalitarian ideals in me, but were forced to say, "Those things can . . . um . . . attract . . . certain kinds of people."

I was floored. How could my parents be so ignorant? If I had disobeyed them, and overcome the improbability of getting a bunch of gaming enthusiasts to the middle of nowhere, my parents would have been proven right, in their noncommittal sort of way; years later I met the nearest gaming enthusiasts, and they were creepy as fuck. It was half a dozen thirty-year-old men in various states of marriage and impregnation with a couple of remaining wives and five or six high-school girls. I wasn't privy to the complex and illegal sexual details, since I got the hell away from them as quickly as I could.

Still, as I ride the subway to my destination, I'm a little excited.

There's no denying my inner geek; it hides in the back of my brain and, when nobody's looking, hopes vampires are real.[*] The rest of me accepted the absence of the fantasy world and got used to living in this one.

But at the comic con . . . maybe the mass consciousness of fantasy obsession creates its own kind of fantasy world. Not an actual fantasy, but the kind of alternate social norm that's occasionally achieved in underground raves and secluded goth clubs, or Simon's Rock. Maybe this will be a shadow of my long-abandoned dream world; the soft space between living and wanting, the place I really belong.

---

[*] My inner geek is very close with my inner goth.

This is also worrying, because if it's true, my girlfriend will dump me.

2:20 p.m., Midtown

I get off the train, and, after a couple of minutes of getting my bearings, go the wrong way. I realize this when I hit a Starbucks I've never seen before, with a revolving door, which I've never seen in a Starbucks. I step in for a short coffee.*

The line is unusually obnoxious, even for a Midtown Starbucks. A couple in front of me is debating over the pastry display a full eight feet from the customer-free register. When the cashier finally drops a passive-aggressive "I can help you over here," they continue to debate for about fifteen seconds. Behind them are a couple of flaky girls. The guy who decides to help them flirts awkwardly for the duration of their order. When he gets to me, he pauses to stare at a tall redhead on her way out. His eyes follow her out the door, then he says, "Damn, that is a fiiiine redheaded lady." It's a painfully self-conscious and amateur composition in misogyny. I crook exactly one third of my mouth and place my order.

I spend the next two minutes trying to decide if the counter guy reminds me more of the geeky kid from *Pretty in Pink,* the short kid in *Angus,* or the forensic scientist from *Dexter* who everybody thinks is a pervert. I'm so preoccupied with all this that I walk out the revolving door without milk

* $1.74

or sugar, and have to do one of those embarrassing full rotations back inside.

Between going the wrong way, the Starbucks, and stopping to write this description of events, I'm another twenty minutes down. I should be at the convention by three. It ends at seven, so depending on the line, I'll have four hours of entertainment. The ticket was forty, so I'll need to get at least ten dollars of entertainment an hour. I remember how much I hate lines, and reflect on what a terrible reporter I would make.

3:00 p.m., Convention Entrance

I have arrived. There was no line, and I have an official-looking piece of plastic around my neck. Now I need to locate the Knobelsdorf and a beer, in reverse order.

3:25 p.m., Food Court

This place is a madhouse. There are tens of thousands of people here, about half of them costumed, from full ghostbuster to generic schoolgirl and/or kitten. Watching them, I'm surprised at how most of them aren't doing anything. Some are passed out; the rest are either taking pictures or hamming for the cameras, or throwing compliments at one another. The compliments are mostly limited to "Awesome sword," because, even here, "You look like an underage theme prostitute," appears unacceptable, and it's the only other option.

I'm in line for what claims to be a place selling Brooklyn Lager, which is listed under imported beer. I'm positive that

Budweiser—the only beer listed under domestic—made a longer trip to get to Manhattan. This line is substantial, and slow moving. No sign of the Knobelsdorf.

After twenty minutes in line, I'm told they don't have any beer because of a bureaucratic error, and I'm sent around the corner to another place that turns out not to have beer. I'm parched, so I buy an apple juice.* That place tells me to go to the third floor.

I don't know which floor qualifies as the third floor, since I'm two floors below ground level, but I start heading up. I ask a few people where the beer is, but nobody seems to know. Finally, as the last person I ask says, "I really don't think they have alcohol here," I realize I can see a shelf of Heineken over his shoulder. I thank him and weave my way toward the shelf.

There is no one else trying to buy this beer,† and they don't even bother to check my ID. I realize for the first time that many of the smokers I saw outside probably can't buy their own cigarettes. I also realize I could theoretically have had this beer an hour ago.

4:10 p.m., Feature Area

I go for high ground, for cell phone reception and to observe the Magic: The Gathering group. These kids are exactly the

* $4.00
† $6.53 for the first, $6.50 for the second, no explanation.

same kids I played with in high school, yet exactly the opposite of the kids I played with after college. In its marketing genius, Magic: The Gathering penetrated both the geek market and the stoner market, and the people who give it up at twenty for the video games they can finally afford are immediately replaced by the people who want to look at pretty pictures and can't afford anything. Still no sighting of the Knobelsdorf, so I make my way down to the feature area.

The only comparison I have for navigating the feature area is trying to get on the 6 train during the morning rush hour. Each step is fought for. It is a solid mass of people; the smaller girls are being protected by their boyfriends. I would compare it to the feeling of being fifteen rows back at a Primus concert, but it's actually worse. At the concert, nobody's trying to go anywhere and they're making room to smoke joints when necessary.

I'm not interested in most of what's going on, which is good, because resisting the flow of the crowd is futile. I pass a dance thing involving a Michael Jackson video game and a bunch of young kids gyrating on a stage in front of it. I think he would have approved.

There are a lot of zombie and vampire video games and paraphernalia; I try to get a closer look, but a confused set of parents is fighting the flow and shouting for their kids, so I get swept up in an eddy and spit into a side corridor, where I catch my breath.

The floor area is about the size of a super Walmart, and every square foot that isn't explicitly roped off is occupied by a person, sometimes two. Screens are flashing, robots are grinding, noise is coming from every side. It congeals into a storm of media; I can barely separate the stimuli, and it all looks fake.

There's nothing for me here, and I'm obviously not going to find the Knobelsdorf. I don't think I could find an elephant in this room. Everything is a mass of flesh and audiovisual chaos. I escape.

4:42 p.m., Autographs

I head for the PC games area; next to the console and comic book section, everything is painfully tame and quiet. It blends into the art supplies section, which might have interested me an hour ago, but now it's just yet another long column of meaningless color. I notice that camera crews are interviewing all the most attractive and scantily clad girls who are old enough to sign their own release forms. When TV ruled the visual media and there were fewer options, they would have interviewed at least a handful of men, or maybe even someone responsible for organizing the event. Now it's a tongue-in-cheek game of seeing how close they can get to sexual titillation without shouting, "Show me your tits!"

I stumble on the autograph area. Personally, I refuse to accept that anyone deserves money for their autograph more than me, so I wouldn't get one for myself, but I catch a glimpse of James Marsters* and consider getting signatures for my mom and a couple of ex-girlfriends.

The autograph lines are sort of like a reverse slave auction, if that makes sense.† There are forty-foot columns delineated by ropes, each column terminating at a celebrity. The line for Marsters is curling into the main walking area; the line for some guy I've never heard of is two people. If I could get a bird's-eye picture, it would be a bar graph of popularity for B-list celebrities.

I'm getting hot again, and my back is starting to give out on me. I should have brought Tylenol. I see a guy in a Hulk suit about twice his size, and I pity him.

On my way out, I see a steampunk Iron Man costume, and it's amazing. But it hits me that he can't possibly expect to talk to anyone through that helmet, and there doesn't seem to be a way to get the outfit on or off with any expediency. He is here for the cameras alone.

I see a place to smoke a cigarette, and make a run for it.

5:20 p.m., Outside

The people next to me are discussing the latest fashion in shouting memes at people. Screaming "CARD GAMES ON MO-TOCYCLES" at Yu-Gi-Oh! cosplayers seems to have fallen out

---

* Spike from *Buffy the Vampire Slayer*.
† It may not.

of favor. I feel old. Some of the conversationalists are so young I can't determine their sex.

When I was in college, "meme" was a debatable, random name some guy was trying to push on us, and you could argue whether it was valid to even make the effort to come up with a name for "ideas that spread through culture." We may as well drop the issue now, because the latest generation uses it in casual conversation.

As the costumed children discuss the cultural landscape in terms I barely recognize, I realize that cosplay (costume play) has no play at all. Its sole purpose is to perpetuate memes, cartoon fluff, and amateur photography. All that happens is people dress up in costumes and take pictures of one another; it's the desire to make fantasy come alive, warped and abstracted into pure self-absorption on a mass-consciousness scale. The totally immersive and addictive video games two rooms away are nothing compared to this. It's pure narcissism, and not even creative; there's no currency in being obscure or unique. Only the most dedicated imitators of the most popular cartoon and video game characters are approachable over the wall of alienation. In the smoking area, the groups mingle like a high-school dance, meeting only briefly and shyly. It's true most of them are in high school, but many of them are not.

I am in the middle of the apex of sexual submission to commercial branding. This is the most failed subculture of all time, living on mostly because its occasional hot, scantily clad female member is so, so hot, and so, so scantily clad.

While lying on my back, chain-smoking, I finally find the Knobelsdorf. Between the cosplayers and my delirium, he seems like the most normal person I've ever met. I bum a light off him for another smoke. He says he's done well networking for jobs, but has acquired none of the females' phone numbers today, though he got two yesterday through text messages. I tell him I'll need to verify the texts, but I cannot go on to document a mating ritual in person. The crowd makes me feel sick.

I have failed in every purpose, both overt and secret. The truth of the Knobelsdorf's claims remains a mystery, I could document next to nothing of interpersonal interaction in the morass of flash and noise, and I didn't get a sonic screwdriver.

Outside, a man in a Boba Fett helmet is playing the soundtrack from *Amélie* on an accordion. I am at once renewed, and undone.

JOSE ARMANDO VASQUEZ LOPEZ

I got my kid while looking for a bathroom after having one of the more depressing lunches of my life at Port Authority, where I was killing time before my doctor's appointment. Between me and the bathroom happened to be a charming girl with a million-kitten smile and excellent teeth.

"You made eye contact," she said, coyly, "now you have to talk to me."

"I know the rules," I said.

So I walked over to her, and she began her pitch for Children International. I wasn't really listening, so I held my hand up.

"Shh. Just tell me what you need."

I assumed a donation or an e-mail would do and let me continue to the bathroom, but it turned out there was a much more complicated application process to begin a sponsorship. She complimented my handwriting as I filled out my name, contact details, and credit card information.

Then it got a little tricky. I was supposed to choose where I wanted my child to be. I looked at the list of countries, which were universally countries I knew nothing about, except that they were all countries where they supply the child models for commercials about poverty and starvation. She directed me to the "Emergency Fund" checkbox, where they'd just pick the neediest country.

Next, she asked, with her improbably charming voice, if I'd like a little boy or a little girl. This was my exact thought process: *Well, I'd far prefer more women than men in this world, and little girls grow up in the most delightful ways. Do I really want to admit that I checked a gender box on a charity program application because I like having sex with girls? No, probably not. But do I want to tell anyone that I ever uttered the words "I'd like a little boy" in a nonironic context? Definitely not.*

"Uh . . . I don't know how to answer that question."

"That's okay, you can just circle both and they'll pick for you."

Thank God.

I wrapped up the application, thanked her, and went for the bathroom. It was appalling, there was no toilet paper, and there appeared to be a resident population I was getting in the way of, so I left, unrelieved. I pondered that there probably should have been a checkbox for New York City on the application, but that wouldn't really be Children International. It made me feel good about my country—and I'd never thought of it in these terms—that there are charities exclusively dedicated to other countries.

That good feeling lasted until my doctor prescribed me Klonopin, which I probably won't take.

Yesterday, I received the information on my child. They gave me a little boy in Honduras named Jose Armando Vasquez Lopez. He is the cutest little boy in the entire fucking universe and I'll kill anyone who says otherwise.

They sent me a bunch of information on Honduras that made me feel like an asshole for not knowing, but that I've really had no good reason to know until sixteen hours ago. Honduras is the "Land of Paradise and Poverty," which reminds me a lot of Maine, the "Land of Vacations and Alcoholism." Naturally, there is sharp disparity in resource distribution, and a 25 percent illiteracy rate. Clinics and hospitals are overrun. They like futbol. This is all completely abstract to me.

But Jose is different, somehow, probably because I have his picture and family information sitting next to my laptop. Jose was born on June 29, 2001. He's three feet and seven inches tall, weighs forty-two pounds, and his favorite subjects in school are grammar and math. I liked math when I was nine, but hated, and still hate, grammar. He likes playing with toys and cars (I'm not sure if these are toy cars, or if he plays with real cars, which I imagine is difficult at three foot seven), and singing and drawing.

His father abandoned him and his two sisters and three brothers, so he lives with his mother, whose job is listed as homemaker. The family monthly income is one hundred and five dollars. This gives me pause, since I spent more than that closing my last bar tab. He lives in a two-bedroom house with the rest of his family. It's made of bamboo, with a corrugated metal roof and dirt floors. I think about my inability to clean cat litter off my floor with appropriate regularity. Their cooking stove runs on wood. The sanitary facility is listed as "open field."

I cannot express how cleverly and completely Children International slashed through my cynicism. I still don't care about the "starving children in the world," but hell if I don't want Jose to get proper medical care and an education. I want to send him books, and maybe skip a few glasses of wine to send his family another twenty bucks a month. I see him growing up to be a poet or an engineer, a famous athlete, or president of the goddamn world.

The poor have never been invisible or disturbing to me, since I'm almost a socialist in the capitalist lie machine, and I know some people need help, and I've needed help before, too. There's a line of logic saying that you'll need less help if you don't give help, but if that were followed to the letter, only the lucky and the powerful would live, and those people very rarely have anything interesting to say. I've dropped as much as twenty bucks at once for the homeless performers on the New York streets. Do I need that money? Sure, and I'm pathetically broke for the amount of money I make due to habits like this, but if you can argue that someone without a home needs a given twenty-dollar bill less than I do, power to you. I'd like to hear your case. I've said before and I'll say again, if I get to the point where I want to drink myself to death, I hope some passing strangers will help me, and I would help another man do it without judgment.

But that's all a philosophical and ethical stance that I only enact in the moment. I consider caring about the worlds a world away to be a form of false empathy, which detracts from the immediate, interpersonal empathy that would do our species so much more good. That's why this organization is so clever: Jose's a person now, a person to me. I'll get letters from him. I'll see him grow in yearly increments when they send new pictures. Most important, I don't feel like I'm condescending to a person who didn't ask for my help, since the desperation of the situation and the impersonality of the organization managing the transaction eliminates all the awkward and inconsistent etiquette involved in helping strangers.

Maybe the fact that I'm a confirmed bachelor with no intention of having kids, but with a nagging desire to be proud of someone besides myself, suits me to this kind of charity. The stress of having a kid would surely kill me, but the responsibility of feeding my cats and now helping pay for Jose's medical expenses probably do more to keep me functioning than Klonopin ever would.

EXCUSE ME, SORRY, THANK YOU

So I was riding home on the subway, sick, tired, off a hard day's night, which makes a lot more sense when daylight savings turns the best part of the day into another irritating period of vitamin D deficiency.

I was paler than usual, feeling thin and generally unappreciated professionally, and especially unappreciated physically because I hadn't been eating right the last couple of days, and had skipped shaving because I was afraid I'd have a dizzy spell while holding a razor to my neck. The same could be said for showering, so I said it and skipped that, too.

Since I wasn't going to any client meetings or impressing any girls that day, I decided to go full deadbeat and donned my skull-encrusted, super-tight BEER DRINKERS AND HELL RAISERS biker shirt, and threw on my crotch-rocket girls' motorcycle jacket.* To reduce irony and make sure I wasn't mistaken for a hipster, I found the largest, loosest, scummiest cargo pants in my laundry, and went to work.

---

* However you choose to parse that noun phrase, you'll probably be right.

Work sucked, and that brings us to the train on the way home.

About midway home, a kid gets on and does a double take of my visage. Too tired to even put up with single takes, I just sigh and hope he's not afraid of me, or shocked by me, or offended by me, because, really, all I ever wanted was to be comfortable and hot enough to be dateable, so all these things are just layers on the skin, they don't say who I am except insofar as they display the kinds of things I'm willing to display about myself, and everybody should be able to express themselves and fuck you for judging me man, and so on. My head rambled freely and feverishly through all the various identity issues and counterissues that so occupied my college years as I stared fiercely at my magazine.

The kid checked me out a couple more times, and on the way out, I had to get around him, so I mumbled a semiaudible "excuse me" and stepped on his shoe by accident. He said something garbled, I said sorry, and I trudged up the stairs to get to the trudge down the street that leads to the trudge up more stairs to my apartment.

Then, midway through trudge two, I realized what the kid had said, which was, "Nice shirt, man."

"Fuck me," I said. Because there I was having a miserable, self-loathing moment of angst I should be too old for, and this kid comes along and validates my outfit, and by extension my whole tactic for dealing with the day, and almost snaps me out of my whole underage, fever-induced funk, and

I just mumbled sorry because I assumed he was an asshole for no good reason at all.

So dude, if you're out there, thank you. You are awesome, and your shirt was cool, too. Catch me on a better day, but don't compliment me on my shirt on a better day because then I'll just think you're shallow.

DATING 101: ROTATION

About once every couple of years, I meet a girl who is exactly like me, and if I'm single, I try to go to bed with her. I always fail, which suggests unflattering things about me, how I interpret what constitutes personality in others, and how I appear to the world and think about myself, but I'm going to skip all that needless self-reflection because it's one thirty in the afternoon, and far too early to start drinking.

The last time this happened was about three years ago. This was, and is, the only date I've gotten from an online source where my date turned out to be more attractive than the pictures she put online. Less attractive, often, as attractive, sometimes, more attractive: once. I was so stunned I said it aloud on the spot, which was probably my best ever opening line for an Internet date.

Conversation was easy, and as happens when two people are perusing the city's selection of dateables, revolved around all the other people we were seeing. Suited me, though it felt a little competitive when we were going over our reference nicknames for the rest. I can't remember what her name for me was, so it probably wasn't flattering[*] and I think my nickname for her at the time was "the hot one," but since I can't remember for sure it was probably something just as emptily flattering.

The first night she drove me home in a car her father had bought her in some attempt at a vicarious midlife crisis. I can't remember the exact model, but it was the kind of two-seater you buy when you're a comfortable middle-class fortysomething and realize you never got the chance to scare cheerleaders by giving them a ride while drinking a beer and doing a buck-ten on the freeway.

The next date, we did an uncharacteristically romantic[†] outing in the rowboats at Central Park. I was hoping for some solid making out, but no dice. She told me about her exes, who were universally older, dumber, and nastier than I was, so I worried that I just wasn't going to be enough of a jackass for her, but damned if I wasn't going to try.

And this brings us to the fundamental problem with me dating people like me. My breed dates for the thrill of it, so we gravitate toward thrilling people, and thrilling people tend to be unstable if not insane. We are not actually thrilling in the way we date. We give off a slightly dangerous and exciting vibe, but we're not the ones fucking up our lives for the ad-

---

[*] It could quite possibly have been "programmer guy."
[†] For me, and since she was just like me, I assume for her.

venture; we seek other people to fuck up our lives so we can deal with it and get the excitement, yet feel like we've been responsible the whole time. So it's a bit like two wolf hunters meeting on the tundra: they have a lot to talk about, they live similar lives, and one of them may want to have sex with the other one, but eventually they have to get back to hunting wolves. Or having sex with wolves. Or the wolves will eat them. Or something. Forget it.

Where was I? Oh, yes: making out in a school playground. We both jumped the fence before we noticed that the gate was wide open ten feet away. Hopping the fence to a playground at night means only one thing, and that's heavy petting. Unfortunately, hopping the fence to a playground that's still open to the public means another thing, namely that a family of seven can wander in at any time, forcing you to quickly remove your hand from your date's pants to avoid traumatizing a bunch of prepubescent kids. I regret nothing.

I do regret the next date. It opened up with us making out on top of a random car in the middle of Williamsburg, which was sort of the coup de grâce in my New York City sexcapades: I've been applauded by strangers twice for a kiss in a bar, once had "Sex! Sex! Sex!" shouted at me by a bunch of frat kids, been accused of being "lewd and licentious" by a passing crazy in a park, slammed someone against and been slammed against the windows at Spike Hill, probably made crowds uncomfortable at 40 percent of the bars in Williamsburg, broken into a construction site to have sex, and just generally been a huge public slut around the busier parts of Brooklyn and Manhattan. But a full-on make-out session on a stranger's car on a busy street is something I have not, in fact, seen before, so it'll be a long time before I need to get more accolades on my resume.

No, the problem was the half-sigh, half-question she asked me near the end of our pizza dinner at one of the few places in Williamsburg where the staff didn't give me dirty looks. It was "So, Peter. Do you want to date me?"

Here was my exact thought process: *Well, she talks about all these other jackasses in her past and how she doesn't want to get in some bad relationship and she said the other day she was toying with the idea of having a rotation of dates or fuck buddies or something do I have pizza sauce on my chin where's the napkin dammit no I didn't what was the intonation in her voice beer where's my beer take a drink play cool you're too into her she wants to make sure I'm not too into her what the hell kind of a question is that?*

So I said, quote, "No." Beat. "But I'd like to stay in your rotation."

To which she replied, "I don't even really have a rotation," and changed the subject.

Although I didn't realize it at the time, I believe that was the end of it. She may also have just not liked me, but girls who aren't attracted to me or don't like me generally don't spend eight hours with me and let me clean their tonsils with my tongue. In the end, I think she was open to more serious dating,* but in my clumsy attempt to secure exactly that, I informed her that I just wanted to have sex with her and move on, and since I was the youngest and nicest thing she had given her time to in recent months, that wasn't what she wanted from me.

C'est la vie.

---

* Although, whatever-your-name-was, feel free to correct me if you read this.

ACCEPTABLE LOSSES

In a pathological act of self-destruction, I bought *Skyrim* the same week that several hard deadlines were set on the sooner portion of my otherwise sparse schedule. Maybe life didn't seem hard enough. Or I just have no ability to fight impulse buying. Or impulses in general.

For those of you in the wrong demographic or just returning from missionary work in Antarctica, *Skyrim* is a fantasy adventure game. A truly fucking awesome fantasy adventure game. It trumps its competition with its scale and its open-ended structure: you can spend a hundred hours playing out a narrative that has nothing to do with the primary plotline. It is to the usual adventure game what the *X-Files* is to *Star Wars*. There's at least one cave that takes upwards of seven hours to thoroughly explore.* Thousands of characters with names and personalities produce thousands of variations of experience, replete with intrigue, well-written dialogue, and histories. For me, it's better than online adventure games,

---

* As a point of comparison, the original *Mario Bros.* can be completed in less than fourteen minutes.

because you don't have to deal with legions of teenagers who usually have less personality than the average computer-generated goblin.

The lack of actual human intelligence behind the characters I interact with in *Skyrim* does less than you might think to prevent me from creating enough neural constructs around them to care about their fates. Many people are happy to play the game as an assassin, a thief, or a bully, merrily murdering imaginary people for profit and pleasure. I just can't. It's arguable that it's a lack of rationality on my part, or an overactive suspension of disbelief. If I've befriended a scripted algorithm, and another algorithm scripted to espouse mores dissimilar to my own orders me to kill or threaten the former algorithm, I can't do it. Despite knowing that the magnetic switches in my PlayStation's hard drive don't care in any meaningful sense whether they're flipped to a one or a zero, I prefer to keep them flipped in a pattern that preserves the illusion of a friendly shopkeeper.

My friend Viking Shaft—who is simultaneously among the nicest and the most intimidating people I know, served in the Israeli military, and incidentally looks much like the six-foot-three Viking character I play in *Skyrim*—has the same problem. He recounts attempting to complete a mission that required him to kill someone (an algorithm in *Skyrim*. He doesn't talk about his military experience), and he couldn't do it. He turned down all the rewards that could have come with this deed because he empathized with a computer-generated personality. And despite the excellence and depth of the game, these personalities are not even particularly complex: Once they're out of useful or picaresque information, their script loops, and they say the same thing every time you attempt to talk to them, to the point of annoyance if it's someone like a blacksmith, with whom you must deal unto the ends of the game. The ones you don't have to talk to serve no other purpose than to break the illusion of the game as they repeat their one or two lines whenever you get too close, yet Viking Shaft and I can't bring ourselves to reduce their data bits to a less excited state.

Aside from being an instant refutation of the belief that you need a god or a consequence to be moral, this behavior starkly contrasts the behavior I displayed in another game.

You thought I was going to say *Grand Theft Auto,* didn't you? I wasn't, but since I know at least 20 percent of the people reading this thought I would, I can use it to flesh out the point. Despite the ultimate social evaluation of my behavior in *GTA,* I went to great lengths to keep my electronic family and the occasional friend alive. The innocent bystanders who get caught in the plotline are so faceless and obnoxious that they don't register as willful beings in our—admittedly misfiring—empathy sensors. Even on the inevitable berserker sessions, murdering the faceless masses is just a way to get the attention of the real opponent: the police. In a social setup where you are already on the wrong side of the law with no way to get back, the police are your opponents the same way zombies and vampires are your enemies in *Skyrim.* Between

Skyrim and *GTA* I've slaughtered thousands upon thousands of cops, monsters, and other data sets with the "enemy" bit switched on, but I always tried to keep anyone with not explicitly threatening dialogue alive. Even though they were the same digital illusions as the faceless and the murderous, I just felt bad for them. *GTA,* as a point-of-view action-adventure game, is not that different from *Skyrim*; the only difference is that *Skyrim* lets you choose your social and moral allegiances.

The troubling game in question has an entirely different character.

Several times during the highly dysfunctional living situation I shared with my heterosexual life mate, Jake, we would drag our computers into one of our rooms and embark on a six- to twelve-hour session of *Rise of Nations.* This is a real-time strategy game in which you pick a few stereotyped ancient cultures and drop them onto an improbably small chunk of the world and see who wins. There are several ways to win, including building the most ancient wonders and reaching the population or educational limits first, but as anyone who plays these games knows, the complete genocide of every other culture is the most satisfying, and leaves little room to doubt who will write the history books.

Since Jake was much better at this game than I, we settled on us playing against four computer opponents of varying ability. Once we hacked the source code to increase the population limit by a factor of ten and let us build cannon-bearing elephants the size of small villages, we played out wars that, if scaled appropriately and fought in the real world, would have wiped out all life on the planet.

There were a few artificial limits that went into our gameplay. First, the other cultures were going to attack you, early and persistently. Yes, we turned off the possibility of our making treaties with them, but we allied them all with one another, so two friendly cultures versus four friendly cultures was actually way ahead of its time given most of the real world's history. There was also a built-in limit to the amount of knowledge you could acquire; Jake and I preferred to set the end of learning at the beginning of the gunpowder age, since it offered a nice mix of melee battles and thoughtful artillery deployment, and because there's just too much shit going on once you have commandos and helicopter squadrons.*

Since there's a population limit, you had to assign your civilians carefully so you had the military power to maintain total war with four angry neighbors. First you need food, so you build farms. Later, wood, followed by metal, becomes necessary to the war effort, so you maintain the minimum number of farms in order to feed your maxed-out population, then as many people as you can spare from the front lines to work the mills and mines. Found a way to work with fewer

---

* The middle ground was World War I technology, but, fittingly, WWI games always led to fourteen-hour sessions. We invariably gave up, then discussed the game in a muted, hungry, and vaguely shell-shocked manner.

farms? Send the farmers to the mines, where they will be targeted by enemy troops seeking to cut off your metal supply. Resources are primary, since war is fundamentally economic. If it takes a hundred of my troops to eliminate ten of your troops, it doesn't matter as long as I can build eleven of mine for every one of yours.

The battles often concentrate around key strategic pathways and resources. You set up constant streams of military units to die at these points, and have to focus on maintaining the stream, since a break will create a brief weakness and loss of land that you will have to fight to take back, usually with last-ditch methods like drafting a swarm of civilians to delay the onslaught while you drain your resources to build military units in the population gap produced by the dying miners. All of this is textbook warfare. Once you accept the conceit and the terms, it's not particularly different from the real world.

There's just one tactical decision that troubled me, even as I gleefully executed it every single game.

When you start, you work as fast as you can to get to the point where you can build universities. You can build three, and you can fill each of them with six scholars. You save your coins for each one, because having the edge in technology gives you the edge in the war. But, as mentioned, there's a limit to knowledge in the game. You spend everything on reaching that limit as quickly as possible. Then you hit it. Then, your schools are taking up valuable space that could be better used for churches, which increase the national borders, hit points, and attack range of a given city. So you burn your schools down. You're left with eighteen civilian scholars. Depending on how much of the map you've explored and how heated the war has become, you either turn them into militia and send them to the far reaches of the world to die while revealing enemy structures, or you just right-click and execute them to open up population slots for new cavalry.

The bleak callousness of this action was never lost on me or Jake. But since the scholar algorithms were more faceless than the cops in *GTA,* we never hesitated. We weren't playing a person interacting with algorithms imitating simple personalities, we were playing a country interacting with other country algorithms. The entire enemy country had no more personality than a nest of *Skyrim* spiders, and our scholars no more import than the magic potions I drop so I can carry an enchanted dagger back to the first shopkeeper who can afford to buy it.

I am never surprised by the atrocities various governments commit to preserve themselves or grab new resources. I'm more surprised by their restraint, and that restraint only exists because we discovered a way to eliminate all human life and nobody in a position of power really wants to do that. However, they have little concern for the individuals enacting their bids to accumulate power, and were I one of the digital civilians I'd moved from a farm to a mine to the front of a war to die so I wouldn't have to feed him anymore, I'd be itching for the technology to break out of my digital prison and burn everything dear to my mouse-clicking overlords.

The technology is arriving for the angry or insane individual to destroy almost as much as a government. A country never seeks to destroy itself, even if it pursues practices with an obvious terminus. A country eats its land, its neighbors, and eventually its own people because it is a system designed merely to persist. A person is designed for the same purpose, but has no statistical average to support their persistence: A couple of faulty wires will end the game.

Subsuming the importance of the individual to a social goal is the fundamental fallacy that allows for warfare. The abstraction of this process, be it a god or a country or a corporation, distances the debate from the relationships between people that might engender empathy. Corporations, countries, and gods do not have empathy. They don't even make the pretense. A committee or individual dedicated to the abstraction can eliminate faceless strangers to the tune of millions without blinking, because there's no relationship between them and the soon to be dead.

The fear of biological warfare, ever-shrinking nuclear devices, and nanotechnology is justified, because each of these technologies puts the power of a civilization in an individual's hands. Acceptable losses to a country are losses that don't impede its ability to continue as a political entity. Acceptable losses to a person who feels they have nothing left to live for tend to include the whole of the known universe. If every mentally competent person of voting age on Earth were given a button to blow up the world when I started typing this sentence, the world would be gone before I finished it.

If it's not already far too late, now would be the time to start treating our individuals with more respect than our goals and ideals. The moment will inevitably arrive when it will only take one unhappy person to bring human history to a close. Best hope they have relationships and loved ones, and that nobody burned down their school.

MEN GOING THEIR OWN WAY

From YouTube comments to Facebook trolls to the abominable testament to the failure of education that is any set of comments on an FML post, the Internet never ceases to reveal, or perhaps create, new dark recesses of the global human condition. The latest basement grave I stumbled across is Men Going Their Own Way.

You don't have to dig very deep to find men being angry because they don't know how to talk to women, but I was surprised to find a non-*Fight Club* social focal point with its own dedicated forum and a point-by-point manifesto. We'll get to that in a moment.

The forum appears to be a kind of social singularity that feeds on the emotion socially awkward and uneducated men feel at the exact instant they're dumped by the woman they assumed would fix all their problems. This has happened to me, and yes, I've gone through periods of hating women in my life. They lasted a week or two, filled with some bro-love and "I never liked her anyway" conversations, then I remembered I had a job and sixty more years to get through, so I got over it. The path to emotional maturity is long and depressing, but you get there, usually somewhere in your mid to late twenties, or at least you get to the point where you're comfortable with your bad decisions and chemical imbalances and you cope as best you can.

Unless, of course, you decide that the whole job, love, and sex thing is a social scam designed to enslave beta males, and your best bet is to drop the whole shebang and participate in society only as much as necessary to maintain an Internet connection so you can post to a forum about how all women are whores and are going to bring about economic collapse.

It really is that amazing. The sheer volume and consistency of open, misogynistic hatred in these forums inspires a bemused awe in lieu of any other possible response. Before the images on the forum page finish loading, you know you're in for free entertainment when the main menu bar pops up and contains these, and only these, categories: "Fathers, Divorce, Porn, Money, Politics, Women," which seems to sum up the lifecycle of an average forum member as long as you stop halfway through. The last three items hinge on the delusion that they've uncovered some massive, scientifically verifiable disaster around the corner and it's all women's fault, because, you know, taking responsibility for your own shitty life never occurs to a real man. This is how paragraphs like this:

> When I first discovered this forum, I felt the
> some of the same sentiments, but it never de-

terred me from reading the threads here. The more I read, the more I wanted to read and discover the truth. It was like when I stopped believing in religion. Sometimes the truth is harsh, but I never regret learning it.

end up sharing roughly equal screen time with paragraphs like this:

I'd also like to add that the real enemies are the white knights and manginas. Women on their own can't do anything.

and this:

Alright you, here's the deal. Yes, a man who respects himself and doesn't want his dick anywhere near the revolving-cock-door monster your vagina has become will probably be turned off by your man number. Trust me when I say that anyone who would be interested in you now is probably just trying to fuck you, since I guarentee [sic] you have a reputation for being easy. Sorry to say it but unless the guy is the whitest of white knights

and/or VERY pussy starved, you might have
trouble attracting a guy with class.

I assume this guy, writing his response to a girl foolishly asking the Internet for a moral analysis of her sex life, considers himself a guy with class.

This porn forum is oddly sparse, but contains the headline "Internet pornography is creating a generation of young men who are hopeless in the bedroom, according to a woman!" which is met with a slew of "So what? Porn is how I avoid women," and "Screw that, I can still fuck I just choose not to" responses. This is right above the headline, "There are new girls coming every day. Hundreds of them," which, wait for it, is met by "See, all women are whores, this is the best use for them anyway." This pair of exchanges pretty much sums up America's hypocritical relationship with porn, stemming from some men's refusal to consider women people who aren't obligated to have sex with them. See . . . hell, see pretty much everything. It's a bad scene.

Welcome to the five-step program to become a Red Pill man. Yeah, they really went there, the whole red pill, blue pill thing from *The Matrix*. Remember? The movie where the hero is saved by true love's kiss? The kiss from a chick? The chick who could totally take care of herself?

The manifesto is actually on mgtow.com, a different url, and a url which is evidently for sale, having achieved some sort of reputation.

According to them, as long as you believe that your own happiness and interests are more important than social expectations and you make your decisions based on that, you can consider yourself as one of the MGTOW—Men Going Their Own Way.

Well, that seems like sound advice, right? Welcome to

Level 0: Situational Awareness

This level includes men who are aware of the realities that face them in society, and yet deem the risks acceptable to have a go at playing the game. I will only touch briefly on this group, as there are not many of these around, and for good reason—the odds stacked against men having the white picket fence deal are still too bloody high. For the first time in a long while, men are having to filter women based on their ability to shrug off constant bombardment by society to give in to their hypergamous natures (and the same bombardment repeatedly chastises and criminalises men's polygamous natures) and adjustment still has to take place, which may not happen before society at large collapses (yes, I'm that pessimistic).

Every good argument should begin with why disagreeing with it will cause civilization to collapse. Lyndon LaRouche knows it, as does the Tea Party. It's almost as effective as saying dissent will kill your children, which is a gimme due to biological imperatives, despite the collapse of society being arguably worse.

But really, saying you shouldn't be beholden to society's expectations is pretty laudable. You just have to respect certain societal expectations so society can continue to function. Except, because of the expectations of women, any man who buys into the system is a sucker. That's why level 1 isn't some claptrap about figuring out what you want and trying to get it.

Level 1: Rejection of long-term relationships

The MGTOW rejects all form of long-term personal relationships with women, including but not limited to marriage, cohabitation of any sort which might be classified as common-law marriage, picking up for a single mother's children, or any action which might be used in court to turn him into her legal indentured servant.

There is absolutely no way the person who started this movement didn't do it right after a messy divorce.

This is where it becomes obvious that this whole thing isn't about self-actualization at all: it's about fear. Look, I'm all for getting rid of legal marriage. You should be allowed to sort out your financial, medical, and personal arrangements with people you trust with the blessing of the government, without this weird, all-encompassing grab bag of entitlements and restrictions based on ancient traditions. But MGTOW's level 1 is about making yourself invulnerable to the possibility of betrayal, which means not trusting anyone, which means you're so afraid of being hurt you would rather not try at all, which means—you guessed it—you're a coward.

And, in the case of MGTOW, a weaselly little backstabbing coward, because each level has a list of "Resources withdrawn from society." In the case of level 1: (a) Intimacy and commitment that women desire, temporary or otherwise, and (b) State-supported wealth transfers from men to women via the divorce, child support, and domestic violence industries.

(a) "Phil, from the looks of that play, I don't think he was adding much to the game anyway. Even if he hadn't thrown a hissy fit and left the field, the coach would have benched him."

(b) Rats. I'll have to dump all my domestic violence stocks.

Level 2: Rejection of short-term relationships

The MGTOW rejects all form of personal relationships with women, including dating, one-night stands, friendships, etc. Any contact with unfamiliar women is kept strictly professional and at a minimum.

This, of course, is where it goes from ignorant and reactionary but discussable arguments about the state of society, to "I hate women because they didn't give me enough sex or took my kids or didn't shut up when I beat them" territory. It lunges straight into the argument that "Rape laws favor the accuser so all men should be afraid." Hmm. Let's see. I've slept with several dozen women, made out with maybe a few hundred, and dated numbers I can't begin to recall. I have never once been accused of rape, or ever even been afraid of the possibility. What could I be doing wrong here? Wait, I'm not sure I have any friends who've been accused of rape. Or coworkers. Or people I've had conversations with. Or met. Or been told about by friends. That's weird. Maybe I just don't hang out with FUCKING RAPISTS.

I'm not saying men aren't falsely accused. It's awful. But it happens considerably less often than actual sexual assault, and I applaud a society that errs on the side of protecting victims. Since we already err on the side of accusing them of being lying whores.

What have our gents taken from society this time? (a) Beta orbiter benefits to women (chivalry, etc.), (b) Greater loss of intimacy and romantic prospects for women, and (c) A general growing indifference by MGTOWs to women (and an observable trend from men in general, too). Hate is not the antithesis of love, because it implies the one doing the hating still cares to some extent about the hated. The indifferent merely ignores all of this.

(a) This is actually a running theme. The people on this site seem convinced of the beta/alpha distinction between men, and anybody joining the site is a proud beta male, branding themselves as born unlucky and incapable of achiev-

62

ing the sex- and money-drenched lifestyles of men with superior genetics. It's the nice-guy fallacy on anti-steroids.

(b) "I agree, Fred. Oh, looks like he's trying to come back on the field and yelling something. Security's removing him now, sorry for the disruption folks."

(c) This doesn't really seem like something taken from society. This is what happens when you get carried away with your bullet points and don't have an editor.

Level 3: Economic disengagement

Now we descend into the wibbly-wobbly crazy.

The MGTOW refuses to produce more than is strictly necessary for his individual survival. He will do as much work off the books as possible to avoid taxation, and will endeavor to remain in the lowest tax bracket possible without jeopardizing his way of life and acceptable standard of living.

Ooookay.

The first common reason for ascending to this level is sited as "Lack of desire to produce due to being denied a meaningful and socially accepted path to respect within the grasp of the everyday beta man." Or, "Because respect wasn't handed to me, I'm taking my toys and going home."

It's epic. In order to punish society, the beta man is going to stop contributing to it, because society never did anything for him, aside from that whole public infrastructure thing.

Look, I know it's a bum rap when society respects me less because I don't make more money. Actually, no, wait, society doesn't respect me less because society doesn't have any feelings at all, and is just a word for an economic and social structure comprised of individuals trying to benefit from distributed specialization. I don't actually need respect from a thing that doesn't have feelings, I just need respect from the people I interact with more than twice a week. It is true that trends and traditions can strongly affect those relationships, so when those trends are broken, we should totally make everything worse by saying they're unfixable and crash the whole system and let everybody die. That sounds like a reasonable reaction to personal loss.

We done yet? Nope. One more step.

Level 4: Societal rejection

The MGTOW drops out of society altogether. He minimises contact with the blue-pill world and seeks to further his own ends on his own terms. For all intents and purposes, he does not exist. An urbanite might keep to his own apartment, while someone further out may simply head into the wilderness and go off-grid.

Fortunately, enough of them stay on-grid to keep this website hopping.

Here, we get to the Zen beauty of the whole effort. These men are willingly removing themselves from the whole game. This problem is consciously and actively solving itself. It is to

women-hating what Breatharians are to religion. The dogma
eats itself, almost like a whiny asshole running off into the
woods where nobody has to listen to him anymore. It sometimes makes me think that this is a clever joke designed to get
men like this out of the way.* All of this makes me hesitant to
write the next paragraph, in case it encourages them to come
out of the woods to whine more.

A personal philosophy based on failure does exactly what
you think it does. A society that creates reactions like this is a
screwed-up society, and that's a problem, but MGTOW doesn't
really blame society: it blames women. Hence its members
have a huge hard-on for yelling at society and women, basically tying their egos to a hatred of everything that went wrong
in their lives that they didn't feel they could control. So they
say they're dropping out and punishing society because it
didn't provide enough free women slaves to please them,
when they're actually just creating an entire lifestyle based on
the thing they claim not to care about. That they claim wom-
en are starting to wonder where all the good men have gone
and that those men are on this website is a level of self-
deception that can probably only be achieved by dropping
out of society, so good job there.

* And, due to Poe's Law, I'm fully open to the possibility that the whole
site really is a joke, but I've read too much OkCupid user mail to think
that these people are unrealistic portrayals.

Breaking free of problematic social expectations affecting your personal life is not about ducking out of society altogether and ranting about women on the Internet. It's about figuring out how to build enough self-respect and mature relationships to be happy, while avoiding the traps that convince you that you're a slave to social expectations and you have to either toil under them or escape. The MGTOW crowd has so utterly failed in their attempt to live for themselves that they base their lives on that very failure, and recede like whispers into the solitude of the shamefully beaten, trying to matter by not mattering.

FULL DISCLOSURE: RAGE

Given enough general financial and emotional security, my hypothesis machine is going to finalize some remarkable theories with its free time, and I'm going to do something stupid. In theory, I learn a lesson, but I know that all that actually happened was that I made the world around me dangerous enough for the "What are you, stupid?" part of my brain to come back online, and all I've learned is a few details about one particular situation and reaffirmed my knowledge that if my brain can't find something to do, it will start creating stories about the private life of discarded pasta, and that kind of thinking rapidly creates real-world challenges.

This is evident during my morning rage fantasies. Commuting in New York City is not easy. For a smoker, the time between waking and the first cigarette is also not easy. Similar problem for coffee drinkers. Nursing a mild hangover also sucks. These four states of not-at-ease describe the first hour of almost every weekday I've experienced since the turn of the millennium, so it's not a surprise I'm angry every morning. This is perfectly normal. What seems less normal is how a critical mass of small annoyances over my forty-five minutes of transit will turn my internalized rage to eleven, to the point where I start twitching and losing time.* The first few annoyances create simple mental processes like "That was annoying," or "I hate people like that," or "Well, she's tired and hungover too," but if enough of these happen, a categorical shift in my conscious interpretation of my body chemistry occurs. By the time I get to the coffee shop, the imagination all the adults told me to cultivate as a child is curb stomping everyone who's looked at me funny in the last thirty years and garroting slow pedestrians while composing emotionally damaging speeches to irritating coworkers. When I'm reading a book on the train, I'm fine, but you can't really do anything on the walking parts of the commute except navigate. After a decade in the city, navigating is now handled entirely by my situational awareness, leaving the "Hey I'm human, check out my brain go!" part of me without enough to do. Add a stack of withdrawal symptoms and the statistical certainty that at least one of the people between me and Midtown is going to think stopping cold in the middle of shoulder-to-shoulder traffic is a good idea, and rage fantasies become inevitable.

For nagging thoughts that aren't caused by withdrawal symptoms, I've found that although it's true you can't decide not to think about something,† you can sometimes accelerate

---

* Although losing time does shorten my commute, so there's a bright side.
† This is true from a simple programming perspective. Say you want to remove every instance of the word *bandersnatch* from comments people

the thinking process into thinking about something else as long as you do it quickly. Though it is true I've had the phrase "pink elephants" stuck in my head since I started this paragraph, had I not been obsessing over this particular process, I could in theory have produced so much noise in my brain that it managed to latch on to something else and push the elephants out. As an untalented meditator, I can attest that eliminating thought is far more difficult that producing more.

But that kind of practice is exactly what causes the problem in the first place: too many goddamn thoughts. The stream of variously rational and insane thinking that causes what people might call mild OCD is barely under my control because of the habits I've taught myself to deal with them, and these habits resemble what people refer to as ADD. For whatever reason, my brain's not going to stop pumping out this storm of words and images, so I need to have a lot of tracks and switches to prevent any particular train of thought from getting too backed up and turning into a nasty neurosis. Most of the time this works out, except for when I try to

---

submit to a web page. So you write a function like this: replace("bandersnatch", "") and boom: no more bandersnatch on the website. Except now the word is built into the program, more integral to the functioning of the website than anything anyone will ever submit. This is why it's senseless to teach children not to say *fuck*: you're just creating a lifelong obsession for them by building it into their program.

clean and work at the same time. Then I get a little weird and have to go to the bar, but that's not so bad.

SOMEONE BLESS OUR WEIRD FUCKING COUNTRY

By virtue of my father's travel habits, 70,000 frequent flyer miles have put me in the Delta Sky With Diamonds Uber Medallion Lounge X, situated a floor above the unwashed proletariat, where I can compose my thoughts without fear of a peasant rebellion.

My thoughts are that, for the first time in my life, I have a mild trepidation about getting on this plane.

I've never been the least bit afraid of flying. I look forward to it, as when I board the plane, my life is out of my hands, and I can dismiss the illusion of control I pretend to have over my life in order to keep jobs and girlfriends. I read and drink, and don't particularly care if the flight is late, crowded, hitting turbulence, or, for that matter, blowing up. It is one of the few activities I do that completely suppresses my death anxiety, the others being reading, enjoying cheese and wine, playing *World of Warcraft,* and having an orgasm.

I have no fears once I actually board, but right now, the incessant sense of dread conjured by weirder and weirder security protocols and warnings has crept into my preflight consciousness, and I am having mildly paranoid thoughts about the plane exploding. I'm far more vulnerable to this in my nonflying state, since I'm still pretending I can do something about it, even though years of social conditioning have not put me in a position where I could decline to fly at this juncture. So I find myself in the personally abhorrent but traditionally American state of worrying about something I've already decided to do. Unless you are receiving or waiting to receive new information, this is the single most wasteful thing you can do with your brain.* Even Raskolnikov saved the bulk of his worrying for after the fact, which is more practical since if you've done something you shouldn't have, a new plan is in order as soon as possible.

On the subway to the airport, a beggar gave a preamble to his request for money, recapping the "If you see something, say something" warnings an average New Yorker gets to hear three or four times a day. He seemed honest, if functionally insane, but his final sentence was, "The best way to keep each other safe is to watch out for each other." I have a fondness for ambiguous wording; in my own writing, to the agony of former English teachers and current editors, I like to compose sentences that can be taken two ways, both of which might be applicable in the context. "Watch out for X" can be taken as "Make sure nothing bad happens to X" or "Make sure X

---

* Except, possibly, fry an egg on it, depending on what that commercial's metaphor was supposed to be

doesn't do anything bad to you," and though I'm sure the subway man meant to imply the former, the necessary inference of the listener, in the context of terror paranoia, is the latter.

This gray area is near the heart of our social issue with the internal war we're fighting in this country, and it's only gray because we're not explicitly authoritarian. We're free-market corporate, which is almost as bad, but has better restaurants for the middle class.

◆

The second thing I did in Portland, Oregon, was visit the Japanese garden. This has a weird meaning for me, for two reasons. Actually, no; there are two reasons it has meaning, one of them normal, the other one weird. The first reason is I visited the garden two years ago, and took a lot of pictures that might have been good had my camera not been on the lowest quality setting, where even the preview is ugly. The second reason is that all things Japanese instill me with a mix of lust, fear, and pity, at least since my engagement to a Japanese woman whose merits and flaws were equally traumatizing. Regardless, I went with a mission, took my pictures in the rain, and staggered back over the ridge of Oregon hills. At one point in this trek, I broke the zipper to my jeans, and at many other points, I drooled over houses with mortgage payments that were 80 percent of my rent and square footage that was 2000 percent of my apartment, and had a view of the city from their living rooms. Such thoughts were tempered by the inevitable and overdue earthquake gathering stress off the coast, where it will someday snap and bring the finest houses in the Northwest tumbling down into Portland like so many dice.

The walk was long, but worth it, in exactly the sense that most walks through Manhattan are not worth it, since walks in Manhattan are obligatory, and involve navigating obnoxiousness for want of arrival, while long walks through driving-oriented landscapes are by choice.

The fourth thing I did in Portland was have dinner with an old friend. That sentence is two-thirds false: I did more than one thing in between, and the "old" part of our friendship consists of me awkwardly hitting on her for four hours in 1997. The new part has been much more fulfilling and pleasant, since we can reminisce about the same people and times without having any personal history to avoid in conversation.

The second thing we did together was walk past the tree-lighting ceremony in downtown, where the FBI was conducting a sting operation on some whack-job kid who wanted to blow up a bunch of Northwestern hippies. It's hard to argue with the sentiment, but I'm glad I didn't get blown up, and now, all of a sudden, we're back to terrorism.

Yet this story is just funny for me, because I didn't get blown up, and didn't have to assist my old friend, who's a doctor, in picking up entrails and saving half-blown-up people. The kid who wanted to blow us up is a poster child for people who want to demonize non-white Americans: His eyebrows alone bespeak the killing of babies. He will claim he was entrapped, he will remain a psycho teenager, and he will spend the rest of his life in a dark prison as both a victim and perpetrator of ideological warfare. I think about how young he is. I think about how youthful passion can be directed at anything, for reasons stemming from sex and branching into the most psychotic of abstractions. His life has been reduced to a godsend to both the people who want to instill fear and the people who want to use fear to control people.

While looking for dinner, we skipped a slew of high-end restaurants, I because I was tapped for cash, she because she budgeted for obscure beers the same way I budget for average wines in Manhattan. A software engineer and a doctor go to dinner together. They can't afford it. The delights of excess are just too tempting to budget sanely, and sanity seems an easy sacrifice amidst the crazies.

I'm reading *Hirohito and The Making of Modern Japan*, a biography of the Japanese emperor during World War II. The government was torn between corrupt politics and the mandates of an ancient code remade for the purposes of the empire and the military. It mentions that most of the people weren't buying the "emperor as god, people as subjects of the divine will" political line. Most people were just running their farms. The beauty of the Japanese garden, precise down to the pattern of the water running over rocks, the fear of my own emotional reaction to the Japanese culture, the horrors committed by a nation one-upped by the horror wreaked by the theory of a shy physicist, and the history of politics spun out of control, all seem separated by chasms of nothing in particular.

♦

If you're a New York City smoker, the most frustrating thing about the Atlanta airport is that there's no place to smoke. We'll take the cosmopolitan attitude toward smoking in enclosed public spaces, because after all we're such forward-thinking people up north we can scoff at the laws of the people too weak to take care of themselves while we applaud the forward-thinking legislation. But what we really want is a cigarette, and that's what the South is supposed to provide for us, while it supplies a solid chunk of Americana for us to mock.

If you're a New York City smoker who's lived in the South for a spell, the most surprising thing about the Atlanta airport is remembering that, for all your vast superiority, the South is full of people with much better manners than you. You feel immediately embarrassed, not for anything you've done, but for what you will inevitably do to offend someone. The scary part is that it's not like another country, or even England or Canada: This is your own country. You should know how to act. But you don't. Everybody is unfailingly polite, and even as you look around with suspicious eyes for

Bush voters, you can't help but notice the dignity everybody imbues you with. There are always the freaks and xenophobes, but the Southern ladies and gentlemen have survived the bigotry and war, and the dignity of the average nonbigot Southerner far exceeds the dignity of the average city liver.*

Portland, Oregon, now a distant place if not memory, becomes a cosmopolitan oddity: Rich enough to feel like a sub-Manhattan, cold and small enough to house an unrealistic number of hippies. It's lamented for being too white, but that not its fault: It's a suburb masquerading as a city, and close enough to Canada to get away with it without being obnoxious. In fact, the politeness could kill a Manhattan commuter, given a few weeks.

Go to Portland to see America in its tweens.

◆

On the last leg of the flight, a woman asked me to switch seats with her boyfriend, so they could sit next to each other. I hate this woman deeply. She made an unreasonable request, especially since it involved me giving up an aisle seat for a middle seat, between (and I didn't even know this yet) the twins from whatever offensive geek-mocking movie of your choice. One couldn't stop sniffing, and the five-to-ten-second intervals between them had an unpredictability that made me

* Read *liver* however you want.

literally tear pages out of my Hirohito biography. They may have been perfectly decent people, but they will not be my friends in this life.

The woman relied on me being nice to the point of being a sucker, and since I am, she won. More important, and whether or not she knew it, she relied on a system of etiquette that dictates succumbing to neediness, mostly because we inherited the acquiescence of British society without learning the part about what questions shouldn't be asked.

Really, the issue was that I couldn't get a smoke in Atlanta, because the South wasn't uncosmopolitan enough and the government was too paranoid to let someone get some air between flights and I was addicted to a drug I couldn't get my hands on, so it wasn't all her fault. But it was enough her fault for me to shoot her, were I an emperor. It's also quite arguably my fault for succumbing to her request and bitching about it. I have already defended myself, but I would also defend myself on the grounds that once she asked, I had the option of being the bad guy sitting next to her for three hours, or just going to sit next to another set of strangers, albeit in a less comfortable seat. There is a list of better things she could have done. But she asked me to move. And I did. And now I'm home and warm and no worse for the wear.

The system works. Even if she was a bitch.

◆

Outside the airport, I finally get a cigarette. In fact, I smoke two in quick succession, which I haven't done in years. All negative emotions are swept away in about two drags, and I note once more how the smokers are the only happy people getting out of the terminal, because even if there's a cab ride and unpacking ahead of us, we have a moment of chemical nirvana where none of that matters. The line for a yellow cab looked long, so I dismissed the plebeian rat race once again and called a car service.

I reflect on my discomfort with the friendliness of the service industry outside New York City. Here, I have relationships with waiters and waitresses that are entirely based on civility. There's little desire and no need to become friends or acquaintances with people on opposite sides of a business transaction. It's optional, and can be pleasant, but is never expected. Here, we are experts in making basic etiquette both informal and sufficient to get warm fuzzy feelings from one another without taxing emotional resources.

I feel safe in the car ride, even though it's technically the most dangerous thing I've done on the entire trip. My home city is, as always, rife with crime and anxiety. It's both the most and least American place in America, a country of implicit countries that get along worse than most of modern Europe. New York City is its own country, dismissive and fearful of the America around it, and within are five boroughs that judge one another harshly, and each borough is a nest of squirming neighborhoods battling for blocks to hold dimly understood borders. It's only the most vivid show of the fractal pattern of alienation, stretching from the world of nations down to the psychotic thought processes an individual has to maintain to live in Manhattan. Yet the hardest and weirdest and loneliest and most insane people flock to this city, and for all its lore of isolation, nobody stays lonely for long. At a point of critical mass, isolated individuals fuse into temporary families; it happens more, and more quickly, here, in the city of people who strive to be a city of one, than anywhere else. When people are forced on one another every day, and there are too many to kill, they learn to get along, and the effort it takes makes most other concerns not worth thinking about.

A fascist police force helps, too.

THE VIEW FROM UP HERE

There's a sense of achievement in hiking to the top of a mountain when you're out of shape that healthy people will never understand. I didn't understand when I was in shape, or when I was a child with an unrealistic amount of energy; it was just a long walk to a view I'd seen before, and I outpaced my family so badly I usually had time to smoke a couple of cigarettes before they caught up. Now I have to take breaks I used to think were pointless just to wait for my pulse to slow down and to convince myself I wasn't going to have a heart attack. After eight years of not climbing anything more challenging than a six-floor walkup, getting a few hundred meters over sea level without the aid of jet fuel feels like winning a death match against a tiger. You didn't just conquer the mountain,* you conquered your creaky joints, your pounding heart, your aching lungs, your bad back and your predilection for thumbcentric exercise.

---

* If mountains could think, I imagine they'd be amused at our notion of "conquering" them.

After almost giving up twice, I decided it would be too embarrassing to make it three-quarters of the way up only to turn ass and mope home complaining of the weak heart my doctor has patiently informed me, several times, I don't have. I broke through to the bare top of Pemetic Mountain with a kilometer to go, said, "I can do this," forgot about the dramatic up-and-down nature of the remainder of official trail, and tried to do the rest of it in one go, in the noonday sun, with maybe three ounces of water left.

Halfway through this misguided venture, I noticed in my delirium a small mossy area under a jutting granite shelf. It was no more than an eight-inch area, but I started to imagine little people living under it, then I scaled it up like a fever dream and I saw the fantasy kingdom of Eyerlaiden, and the forest cavern above the Starfalls (a trickle of rainwater heading down the mountain, about six orders of magnitude less impressive in nonheatstroke terms than a stream), where a thousand years before, the young princess Gaim had opened the throat of the last unicorn, driving magic from the land and the sorcerers' power from the gates, forever ending their mad quest for ascension.

When I snapped out of it, I realized that when I was a child, this was how I saw the world all the time. The grand vistas were too much like maps: I didn't have the brooding ennui attempting to connect my tiny self to the vastness of the horizon. The stars were not yet made terrible by the intellectual grasp of their size and distance. My fascination was with the little and the mundane; uncomplicated structures onto which I could paste my imagination. The box was always more interesting than the toy, and why get a plastic sword when a branch could be a sword, a wand, and a gun as the situation warranted?

As new information poured in and I had to deal with increasingly complex social computation, sticks became sticks and rocks became rocks. It wasn't that I couldn't dig into to the possibilities of barely articulated forms, I just became busier with the over-articulated systems of knowledge and thought I had to start dealing with on my way to self-sufficiency. * It's a much harder thing to do, and the knowledge acquired makes it more and more difficult to go back to these inner worlds.

Some students attending my pre-pre-pre-pre-alma mater once tried to get a game of Calvinball going. This is from *Calvin and Hobbes*, and you make up the rules as you go along. This works as a literary device and if you're a child who doesn't know very much about the world. Children aren't more successful at the game because they're more creative; they get away with it because they're ignorant and not that creative, so they're limited in the random rules they can bring up and how they can defend them. The small amount of physics and logic learned by mid to late teens makes the game unplayable because it's too easy to twist around made-up rules ad infinitum, and college-aged attempts to get the

---

* And after thirty-four years, almost there.

game going inevitably die out. Creativity and originality are not about thinking outside the box, they're about building your own box and working your free-association skills within it.

That said, the innumerable boxes lined up for young adults to jump in and out of on the way down the paper trail to a living wage create the illusion that some creative power of the mind is lost; that the imagination, busy with navigating the puzzles of culture, was crippled along the way. This isn't so. It's becoming more powerful every day. You just use it more often for extrapolating regret, stoking anxiety, and dealing with romantic relationships.

I don't know anyone who hasn't seen an attractive person on the street and imagined the sixty-year story of their meeting, dating, struggles, marriage, children, and death in less than two seconds. Ten seconds, and the imagination's gone through the equivalent of two romantic comedies, complete with alternate endings. Before the face is forgotten, there's usually enough material for a four-season sitcom. This is the same mental process that imagined fantasy kingdoms in its youth. When the hormones kicked in, it got busy with sex.

So of all the things found in relationships that aren't commonly found elsewhere, this reinvigorated access to imagination through the details is one of the more engaging elements that lead us to think of love as autonomously transcendent. Few other situations create as intense fascinations with something as simple as a particular section of un-demarcated skin, where the decision to touch or not to touch becomes a boundless source of stories. The handful of consciously accessible bits of information we get from the movement of a lover's eyes can focus the entire mind on the search for the meaning of those movements. Each detail of a relationship spins off new jungles in the imagination, navigated by necessity and at peril, with limitless possibility.

The top-down view of a relationship is checkers compared to the irreducible complexity of experiencing it. For the purposes of communication and therapy, you can sum up a relationship in a few paragraphs and it will fall into some pattern with statistically predictable outcomes.[*] When you get away from a relationship, you can see the broad features of it, good or bad, and know why you had to get out of it or were an idiot for leaving. Friends not in the relationship can see it all the time, and may make occasional observations that affect the course, but of course they can't really understand what's going on: The conscious mind is pinning the needle on all its most powerful faculties to experience the relationship and its potential paths, and all that complexity is wrapped up in the most subjective parts of individual experience. Romance is a mountain of stories told over inconspicuous details, and the climber navigates the path, while the distant viewer sees only the mountain.

---

[*] Researchers have found they can predict the whether a marriage will last after watching a video of the couple interacting for three minutes. With garbled audio.

We communicate in distant views. People are impatient with long explorations of others' internal worlds, and as more of our time is taken up having to explain ourselves to other people, a metaphorical succinctness becomes useful. It sounds as if our brains are lacking rich imaginative worlds just because we don't want to bore one another with them, and it feels as if our brains lack internal worlds because we're busy with the outside world. Creativity and isolation are not linked by accident: Dedication to the internal is more likely to produce something unusual to the rest of the world.

So despite the feeling that the world isn't as fun as it was when we were kids, the imagination didn't go away, and kids don't have more of it. The imagination is busy navigating adulthood, dealing with existential uncertainty, and coming up with fictitious explanations for its own demise.

FORMATIVE MOMENTS

On a March night in 1999, soon after the temperature dropped to the point where the body no longer registers cold and all exposed skin merely reports pain, I tossed my broken ATM card in the snow, lit a cigarette, and prepared to die.

I was being melodramatic. I could see the silhouette of a house across a field; if anyone was home I could wake them up and beg for a few hours of heat. In the moment it seemed like another doomed effort. They'd probably shoot me: This was post-Columbine, and everybody over thirty was still worried about the mythical Trench Coat Mafia, who would have dressed exactly the way I was dressed at the moment.

I looked to the black-on-black horizon above gray-blue snow, lit by little more than my optical nerve's desire for contrast. Why not die here? Didn't seem like there was much to live for anyway.

◆

The short version is, "Yeah, I almost got married. Then she slept with Scotland." It's the version that gives a shock and gets a laugh, something you can give out to satisfy curiosity. It prevents them from asking more and you having to recall the cacophony of evil thoughts too complex and dark to explain.

In 1998, I somehow managed to find a girl with a set of problems perfectly tuned to exacerbate my own problems, and convinced her to date me.

I don't believe in love at first sight. When I first saw Her, I thought She was hot. She was dressed in red and black lace and velvet and fishnets and looked like She'd dropped out of one of the fantasy novels I used to read to forget that I couldn't get a date. It was my first week of college, and I was an obnoxious sketchball. A lot of people knew what I didn't: I was an overly eager, up-and-coming drug user who might well get other people busted because weed was still daring and cool, and underage drinking was something you had to hide from the folks. I saw Her leaning against the wall outside the student union, and managed to talk to Her because it was a three-hundred-person hippy school, and you could chat up anyone, no matter how gorgeous or depressed they appeared to be.

We hung out. She was good-looking, sure, but tons of people were good-looking there, by some freakish demographic phenomenon. I had a new infatuation every week. I started going out with Lauren.

Lauren was nearly blind. Lauren was a twelve-year-old girl trapped in a fourteen-year-old's body that just happened to be eighteen. I was seventeen. Lauren was the sweetest person on

Earth, not because she tried to be sweet, but because she was agonizingly naive. Everybody at the college gave her shit, because no matter how much they pranced around in their little "I'm so different I'm cool" fantasies, Lauren was actually different, hence difficult to deal with. She thought and reacted to everything in a way that was just a little off, and nobody could relate to it. It's hard to shrug off the delusion that looking into someone's eyes is a useful way to judge them, and this was impossible with Lauren because one of her eyes always looked like it was following a confused insect flying behind your head. She laughed suddenly and evilly at things that people didn't realize were kind of funny until seconds, minutes, sometimes days later. Tiny oddities stack up and make it easier to objectify a personality and dismiss a way of thinking you don't feel like you have the time to unravel.

I used Lauren repeatedly and cruelly. I confused her with bullshit whenever I broke up with her, to alleviate my own guilt, and to make it easier to crawl back when I got lonely. But I couldn't be tied down, or honest or anything, because I was in my prime! I was fresh off the Maine coast with a back full of sailor's muscles and a cock full of pretension. A real man always remembers that, ultimately, it doesn't matter how smart or nice or good-looking you are: You are judged by what you ignore, and the people you hurt. That's how you win.

I didn't want to hurt Lauren. I did. And I forgot about it, because I was falling in love with Her.

◆

Jeff and I were at a truck stop diner twenty minutes out of town, at about one in the morning. We had managed not to talk about Her for almost an hour, which was a conscious achievement on my part. Most of my conversations were about Her, and consisted of me finding increasingly defensive excuses for not bailing out of the relationship. This was particularly hard with Jeff because he had a weird obsession with both me and Her. He also had bipolar disorder, and my relationship was the kind of thing he wanted to see work out, as it was not dissimilar to the imaginary relationships he saw himself one day being in.

I was almost having fun until two state troopers came in and started talking about the roads. It was the middle of winter and there was reason to be cautious, so I asked them how bad it was.

They laughed. "We're sure as hell not driving on them."

We took this as our cue to get home. The drive started out easily enough, and I tested the brakes gently. Seemed okay. I pulled to a stop and tentatively put my foot out on the road. If I could have made it plausible, I would have testified that something strong and angry yanked my foot out from beneath me to explain how I managed to fall on my ass with only one leg out of the car.

◆

I talked to Her every day. We'd have fun. I'd relax, and think what a good friend She was. And every day, I fell more in love. I dumped Lauren for the fourth time and moaned about my goth goddess, because She had a boyfriend.

She liked to talk about what a twat Her boyfriend was. He was a little odd—liked to chop down trees with an axe, which the school authorities chose to ignore. Last I heard he was working for the government because he can do things on the Internet that maybe a hundred people in the world can do. Owns a gun. Still hated me, last time I checked. I don't hate him anymore, no matter what weird things he did, because I know She did to him the same thing She did to me.

I finally told Her on some night when we were out driving. She was talking about how She wanted to leave her boyfriend. It was a slow, word-a-minute kind of conversation. She kept talking about how something wasn't there. Something wasn't right. I wasn't old or tired enough to point out that that's how it always is. You stay in a relationship because you've fixed what you can and are willing to put up with what you can't. Or, you stay a relationship because you're addicted to pain and don't trust yourself to run your life alone.

Even if I had known that, I wouldn't have pointed it out. All I could thing about was the way Her hair fell forward when She changed the CD track. The way She smoked, inhaling a little air first, then taking a drag. The way She looked in a velvet vest. The way She smiled with Her whole face. The way She sang. A few notes could make you cry.

Later, when we were together, She drove down a country road at seventy, cranking up a song the radio while singing a different song. Every few seconds, She would turn up the volume, then sing louder, then drive faster.

That night She didn't sing. We drove around the country block, again and again, while different parts of my child brain screamed at each other with faux wisdom and extremely real, thought-consuming infatuation, about whether or not to say anything.

Eventually, we were at Her door, and I took a chance, with a cracking voice.

"I don't know how to tell you this. I'm in love with you. I'll be home when you want to talk."

I wish I could describe the expression on Her face. I wish I could remember being that innocent. I'm definitely not as sweet as I used to be, but I held on to the little-boy thing until eighteen.

I spent the next day staring at the wall. For hours. I was already as in love as I would ever be. Eventually, we met on the bridge in front of Her dorm. We went to Her room.

In the next twelve hours we listened to *Violator,* a best of Fred Astaire album, and *The Downward Spiral* about four times, because those were the CDs in Her three-CD changer when we set it on repeat. Lots of tickling, wrestling, pillows, and endless pauses. It ended with a kiss. Eight hours of wondering, tension, a million things unsaid. A kiss like an entire childhood of desire burning away.

◆

After the goblin yanked my foot out from under me, we took the rest of the trip at about five miles an hour. In town, the roads were fine, so I got Jeff close to his dorm and headed home. In the middle of town I saw a hitchhiker I recognized as a college acquaintance and picked him up, since I could tell where he was walking and it was a ridiculously long walk to take on a freezing winter night. It was another fifteen-minute drive, but I was hopped up on adrenaline from navigating ice for two hours and hey, the roads were fine now.

It would occur to me later that the roads were fine not because the temperature had gone up, but because the sanding trucks hit the population centers before they worked on the country roads.

I realized this ten minutes out, when the front of my car started to drift and I tapped the breaks.

The car spun soundlessly through the night, directly into a snow-covered stone wall bordering the right side of the road. It hit nose-first, but the momentum was all downhill, so it started spinning end around end to the bottom of the slope. I think we did 1080 degrees altogether, but I was a little disoriented.

◆

After thunderstorms, drama, threats from ax-wielding ex-boyfriends, and so on, the school year ended. My grades had dropped. We had spent most of the semester hiding in Her room, which was tricky since She was a resident assistant and the school had rules about being in other people's dorms after hours. But we got through it, with a lot of drugs and sex, and only one pregnancy scare that I recall.

She went back to Baltimore, I went back to Maine. We were both rabidly antitechnology, so there was no e-mail. Just letters. Every week I'd get three or four, and send just as many. Letters with homemade envelopes, woven together out of paper I marbleized myself. I learned more arts and crafts for this girl than I did for every art teacher I ever had. At its worst, I wove a necklace with complicated cat designs out of beads smaller than a guppy's eyeball. Why not? By that point, I could barely read. That was later.

I spent two weeks in Baltimore. It was a haze of sixteen hours a day in bed, break for food, go back to bed. Thirty-five hours of *The Simpsons* and *The Critic*. Tape after tape of MTV. Et cetera. I don't remember separate days, just swimming in and out of consciousness. This was before I'd discovered Morphine, so we didn't have the right music; it was all Depeche Mode and Nine Inch Nails.

She spent two weeks in Maine, which was the same except I had to work and She was deathly sick.

We moved in together after the summer. This was a pretty good deal. I wasn't in school, so I could work part-time to feed the cats. Her parents loved me because I was the first boyfriend that wasn't a heroin addict or a psychopath, so they paid for everything. I was a sugar baby. All I had to do was pretend to have a work ethic thirty hours a week, then go home and drink and smoke and have sex. Movies, movies, movies, late nights, parties. I was set. I did nothing interesting or creative, because why should I care? I was in love! I slept next to my love every night, and woke up, and there She was! I didn't want anything, anybody else, ever. And Her parents were rich, so why worry? We were already talking about getting a house in Baltimore, and, should we think such thoughts . . . getting married? Married? Yes! Married to the perfect woman, in the perfect house, in the city of Baltimore, where I used to live anyway, so it would be like going home.

Of course, there were a few things wrong. She was always put out that I had to go to work. She hardly ever said goodbye; She would just give me one of Her pained smiles on my way out. When I came home with a pocket full of food or change, depending on what restaurant was underpaying me that day, She wouldn't speak to me for half an hour. Six hours a day was too long for me to be away. Because She had no friends, right? I had to be home. There was no one else around. Nobody ever came over. She never did anything outside of school. She felt guilty because I worked and She didn't. Sometimes She would chain-smoke until She was sick, waiting for me to come home. The bad days were when She cleaned. She would spend six hours cleaning, then I'd come home and say, "Wow. I didn't know it looked like this." She would be at the table with a beer, and tell me how She felt worthless because She stayed home and cleaned, and how She didn't support herself, and everything was me or Her parents. So I told Her She should get a job. She found a job doing nude modeling for some guy who claimed to be the art director for *Yellow Submarine.* Maybe he was. It was probably a line. He was a fiftysomething who paid Her forty bucks an hour and said things like, "I don't sleep with all my models." She felt horrible doing it, so She quit, and felt horrible for quitting. We started to fight a lot. Sometimes She would scream. Sometimes She would be sarcastically happy and shout, "See? See how nice everything is?" and sing nasty songs and run around the apartment. She would burst into tears, randomly. Friends stopped coming over. She said mean things about my friends more often, not offhand comments, but confidential admissions about why this person or that person made Her uncomfortable. God forbid I should ever go anywhere without Her. She had nothing to do, and some unnameable thing was going terribly wrong, and I could not fix it, and She needed me to fix it, and She would collapse into me at night and tell me She was afraid without me.

She went to England for Her second semester of that year. I was going to be alone in the apartment. At the time, I feared this as much as I fear death today. We were so dependent on each other, and so hostile to anything that might come into our lives, we had nothing else. We had no idea what we'd do without each other. There was some ideal of love that I thought we had, and that She felt was flawed, and I was trying to fix it, and She really hoped I'd fix it, because She was still miserable and didn't know why, and I was living off the high I got from making Her smile, maybe once a day, once a week near the end. We didn't eat. We didn't talk much. We were afraid, and for a few good days before She left, the fear of being apart drove us together.

◆

"Holy fucking Christ," commented my passenger, cigarette dangling from his lips.

"That was unexpected," I said, with the calm people have when they've subconsciously decided they don't really care about life and have just nearly ended it, creating a feeling of freedom and contentment as the mortal apathy becomes conscious. I got out and checked the car for damage. There wasn't so much as a chip off the paint, so, in the spirit of my just-realized suicidal calm, I drove my passenger two more miles before heading home.

I resumed my earlier five-mile-an-hour strategy, which got me about five miles back to town. The fear of death started to seep back in as I realized what I was going to have to navigate: steep, repeating hills, often peaking and valleying at sharp turns bordered by hundred-foot sheer drops into forest ravines. Driving consisted of working my way up a hill, descending with a hand on the parking brake, and meditating on all the things I had yet to do in my life.

◆

For the first month and a half, She called me every night, crying about how cold and lonely She was, and how She never went out, and had no friends, and didn't like the other Americans, and how She missed me and wanted to come home. She started drinking a lot, because it was legal for Her to drink over there. Then She called me less often. I thought, good, She's feeling better. Then She told me about Steve. She told me not to worry about him, he's just a friend. I said, okay, I won't worry, even though I hadn't been worrying, but now that She told me not to, I was really fucking curious about Steve. He was Scottish. She liked Scottish accents. He was a cokehead, and tried to get Her to do coke. Great. Just what the hundred-pound girl needs.

I went to visit Her for my birthday, courtesy of the girlfriend's-mother fund. That was okay. She didn't want to be touched. I couldn't fuck Her. I couldn't kiss Her. I couldn't hold Her. She wasn't feeling well. "Fine, I don't need to, I can love you without any of that. I don't care if we never have sex again, I still love you." She cried when I told Her this. I couldn't do anything right. I wasn't British enough to understand London. Come on, I know not to talk about soccer and not to make fun of the queen, those are the only real survival skills you need in England. We fought, about nothing. My birthday was coming up. She didn't want to talk about that for some reason.

I found out later She was making out with Steve in the kitchen, across the hall from where I was sleeping, two days before my birthday. I found out by reading Her diary, though when I told Her, I lied and said I saw them going at it.

She told me the next day that we shouldn't talk to each other until She came home. If She came home. She told me this in a train station on the way to the airport, on my birthday. I threw up in the bathroom, where some guy asked me if I cared for a buggering. He was pretty insistent until the cops kicked him out.

Somehow, I still loved Her.

Somehow, we parted on a good note. I don't know how we got from A to B on that one. And I had a twenty-nine hour birthday, including sixteen hours of travel. Don't think anyone wished me a happy birthday that day except for Luke and Aime, to whom I wish I'd been a better friend, because they were the ones telling me to get my fucking act together.

She didn't call much after that. I called Her quite a bit, which resulted in a thirteen-hundred-dollar phone bill I never paid. When She called me, She called drunk. She often called when my friends were over and I was actually having a good time and sometimes not even talking about Her. My favorite call was when She called to tell me She was really upset because She had hurt Steve. I don't even want to admit that I still considered Steve an unimportant threat. I told Her to tell me what She had done. Oh, She went to a bar with Steve, and ended up sleeping with the bartender. This hurt Steve, because whenever they tried to have sex, Steve couldn't get it up. And this right after She had fucked Steve's best friend.

I kept up the facade while She called me about new drunken conquests. When I called Her back the next day, She usually said She couldn't remember calling me, or what She said, so we'd go over it all again. I quit my job. I slept until two, woke up, felt good for about two seconds, then remembered who I was and what I was doing. I smoked two packs a day. I drank a lot. I smoked a lot of weed. I played video games until dawn. Most days, I didn't go out, and nobody came over. I hated dawn. I hated those fucking cheery birds. I would be miserable for most of the day, until night fell, and I could defend doing nothing with my life by saying all the stores were closed and I couldn't look for a job now anyway, so I could get stoned for the rest of the night and play video games. Usually I would miss Her for a couple hours. Then I'd be stoned or drunk enough to zone out to old *Red Dwarf* episodes for a while. Then I would hate Her, violently, until about three in the morning. Then I'd get the high from being awake all night, and I'd go for a walk, get some fresh air, and think, "But I'm in love, so none of this matters, She'll come home, and we'll fix it, we'll fix it!"

On more rational nights, I would be thinking, "I could go. I could just leave. Get the hell out. Fuck the apartment. Take my cat and run. I can go." I would feel free until I got home and remembered my willpower and my balls were still in a drawer in England, next to a beaded bracelet She refused to wear.

At one point She told me to cheat on her because that was the only way I would understand. Understand what? Just do it. Fine. I did.

For some reason, despite being a near-hopeless wreck, I managed to turn on the charm for exactly forty-eight hours, at the end of which I was in bed with a sixteen-year-old red-headed dancer who was argued to be the cutest, nicest girl in town at that point. Great. But I couldn't do it. Why? First because I couldn't get my girlfriend out of my head. Then, as the drugs sank into my system, and the madness of total self-hatred hit home, I decided this girl was my angel savior, and I didn't want to fuck it up. So I acted really strange around her for a couple days and she told me to fuck off. She was nice about it.

I wasn't making any friends right about then. I was dele-gated that category of weird guys who pop up now and then but don't talk to anyone.

I got a job in an institute for the profoundly mentally and physically disabled. Third shift, from eleven at night to seven in the morning. I sat for eight hours with my partner, who had been working there for a while and was starting to lose it from sitting up all night listening to inhuman screaming and cleaning shit and blood off the walls while patients ate their diapers. Probably the wrong job to take right about then, but it paid ten bucks an hour (back when cigarettes were two-fifty a pack), and most of it was watching TV.

◆

I eventually came to a hill I couldn't climb. I would ease my way up, then, midway, the car would start pirouetting back to the bottom. I tried three times with no success. I couldn't drive faster, as the wheels would spin out if I did more than suggest the car should be moving forward.

Eventually, I backed up the hill behind me as far as I could, then coasted up, laying on the gas as much as I could to get momentum. This worked.

I had to do the same thing for the next hill.

And the next.

On the one after that, even this didn't work.

I tried twice, but had become familiar enough with ice-incline friction dynamics to know it was futile. I got as far up the hill as I could, pulled the parking break, got the ice-scraper out of the trunk, and chipped two fifty-foot tracks in front of the wheels.

◆

Nobody ever said this to my face, but it was possible I was hell-bent on fixing my relationship because of the relationship I couldn't fix.

Maybe a month before she left for England, I went home for a few days to visit old friends and my parents. They asked me how things were going. I said okay, because they were okay. It was cold. I saw everyone I wanted to see, and came home stoned and cheerful one night because my girlfriend had finally decided to hang out with some of my friends and was having a good time on Her own for once. I decided that once I got home, I would apologize to Lauren, and try to reconcile, because she really was the sweetest person I'd ever known, and she deserved more than the "I'm too dangerous for you" bullshit good-bye she got from me.

When I got home, my mother told me to call my apartment. It was a little stunning that my mom was still awake at one in the morning. She sounded worried. Said I had to call now. I did, and Luke was on the phone. It would take too long to explain how close a friend Luke was, but it was still a little surprising to hear him pick up in my apartment.

"Luke? What's up?"

"Peter?" He sounded strained.

Jesus Christ, is She okay what the hell's going on I'm too stoned to handle something like this, Jesus, where is She, I love Her, I love Her, She has to be okay, we were going to get married—

"You didn't hear?" said Luke.

"Hear what?"

"Lauren's dead."

I was empty. I couldn't speak. I didn't cry. I didn't scream. I was empty. I just thought the words over and over. Lauren who? Lauren's what?

It didn't sink in then. I don't think it will ever sink in. It hasn't sunk in now, as I'm writing this. It still hurts too much to let it all the way into my thoughts. I keep it in my stomach, where it makes me sick sometimes, usually in January or February, when it's dark and I'm sleeping alone.

"How?"

"She killed herself."

"Oh."

"Are you okay?"

"I don't know."

He put my girlfriend on the phone.

"Peter?"

"Hey."

The first thing She said was that we shouldn't think of ourselves, we should be strong, we should try to help other people.

Help who? How many people had been nasty to Lauren? I only knew one or two other people who had ever said something nice about her when she wasn't around. Who had given a fuck that she was alive? Who had ever tried to help her or hang out with her? When we went to the wake, I saw a hundred people who were there because they were guilty about treating her like shit. They said stupid things, and laughed as if they were trying to break tension and hide pain they didn't feel. I saw her old roommate, who once got props from her friends for bitching Lauren out about being weird. She said she always respected Lauren. They played a song that Lauren didn't know, because no one knew what Lauren liked, and they had to play something since they had the damn piano.

I was still empty.

My girlfriend never talked about it, except to say, "I can't talk about it." Who was I supposed to talk to? The girl I lived with, maybe? The girl I gave everything to, gave everything up for? No, She couldn't talk about it. She convinced me to be strong. And then She left.

◆

On the next hill, I realized I didn't have to chip full tracks, just foot-long areas about five feet apart, which would let the wheels catch periodically.

On the next hill, the ice scraper broke, so I started going through my wallet. My student ID, library card, and ATM card got me over that hill.

On the next hill, my ATM card broke and I gave up. I had nothing left with which to scrape, and the temperature had dropped so the ice was getting harder. It was three in the morning, I was almost out of gas, I was seven miles out of town, it was thirteen degrees out, and I only had a light coat. I started wondering how long I could jog in place, and if it would be long enough to keep me from freezing to death.

Ten minutes after this, a sand truck came down the road, backward, so it could sand in front of itself. It was a relief in that I wasn't going die, but frustrating that all of my efforts amounted to an inefficient and dangerous way of achieving what I could have achieved by letting the engine idle and reading a book where I'd spun out two hours and six miles ago.

I got home and left this recording on the answering machine: "Hello, this is Peter, please leave a message, but I almost died at least twice tonight so I may not get back to you for a while." This was a morbid joke meant for my friends, and a passive-aggressive plea for sympathetic affection from my girlfriend.

I missed on both counts, because my friends didn't call, so the only message I got was, "What did you do to my car?"

◆

She called me one day to break up with me. She had gone to Steve's house and said She didn't want to be called or contacted. That's what it said on Her answering machine: "I'm going to Scotland for a few days. Please don't try to get in touch with me, I need to be alone to think things over." But She called me, and told me She was going to live in New York with Her best friend for the summer while I looked for a new place. This was the first time I ever told Her, "Fuck you."

I cried for about three hours. I finally called my dad, who calmed me down and told to get the hell out of the apartment and think about being free.

I moved out two days later and ended up sleeping on a friend's couch for the summer. She came back and stayed in the apartment with Steve. The day that happened, I couldn't sleep. I fell asleep at work, and my coworker ratted me out and I was told to go home. I couldn't take care of my cat, so when I finally went back to Maine, broke, missing most of my things, weighing 117 pounds, having lived off peanut butter and cigarettes for a summer, I left my cat with Her. She took him to Baltimore when She gave up and went home. I'm pretty sure he's dead now.

A week after I was told to go home from my job, I was called in to "talk about my employment." I started walking there from my apartment barefoot, since one of the smellier problems with not having any money is you can't wash your socks. A former classmate, who was doing much better than I, pulled his car over and gave me a lift to the meeting that I thought was going to get me my job back. With my tattered jeans, long hair, and bare feet, I'm surprised they let me in the building.

I sat down, not even realizing how ridiculous I looked, and the woman on the other side of the desk said, "How do you feel this is working?"

This was not the question I expected, so I rambled through some sorry-please-don't-fire-me boilerplate for about twenty seconds, until she cut me off with, "We don't feel this is working."

It's entirely possible they weren't going to summarily dismiss me before I walked in barefoot and six days distant from a shower, but that's what they did.

I started walking back to my friend's couch. I spent my last dollar on a bottle of water at a farmers' market, which took the edge off. I drank most of it and poured the rest on my feet, since I was walking over blacktop and it was just over a hundred degrees. In the middle of the highway bridge, I leaned on the barrier and pulled out my last cigarette, not knowing where the next one would come from. Halfway through that cigarette, I thought, *I'm not dead yet.*

I can't say the next two months of homelessness were all fun and games. But at that moment I was broke, hungry, heartbroken, fired, and getting first-degree burns on my feet. Everything I'd spent the last year working for was gone forever, and I had to start over. And it was the one of the best moments of my life, because I knew I would live through the day, and through the one after that. I had met my opponent, and my opponent was the awful shit that happens despite, and sometimes because of, my best efforts, and I knew that in the end my opponent was going to win.

But I knew I was going to fight.

◆

I don't believe there are singular moments in life that make us vastly different people depending on how they play out. The ego-driven narrative we think of as ourselves likes to pick out self-altering events, but the brain supporting that story is very good at averaging out the randomness of life and sustaining a personality that will be pretty much the same regardless of circumstance. Built over that personality are rationalized principles based on anecdotal evidence with a smattering of fact-checking.

If all this hadn't happened at the end of my teenage years, I wouldn't be a fundamentally different person. I might weigh more, or be less addicted to cigarettes, but I doubt it. I might not have gone through my infantile woman-hating stage over the next couple of years, but the experiences and socializing background noise that formed that attitude would have outed itself in some other way before it was properly shot down by my more adult peers and elders.

I appreciate the visceral evidence that the universe did not love me. The beginnings of my eventual conclusion that the universe was a cold and uncaring place were conceived the first time I saw *Crimes and Misdemeanors*, so I was well on the way to that before all this, but seeing the theory in practice may have jump-started the impulse to not accept my life as it was, and derailed some acceptance of purpose beyond my control. To this day I hear even my most anti-Christian friends spew nonsense about failures just being the universe telling them they weren't ready, because the universe has a plan and cares for them and reasons and love, etc., without for a moment realizing this is the same thinking people invoke to excuse their life not being what they thought it would be, encouraged by institutions profiting from apathy to get poor people to shut up. I can still hear a perverse argument from them along the lines of "Well, the universe cared enough to demonstrate it didn't care," but hunger is a handy memory for short-circuiting this kind of logic.

I discovered that what love there is in the world is not a force that will ford all the rivers of our discontent. It's an agreement, and a sweet vulnerability between two people that tends toward decay. It's a fragile thing that takes a lot more work than hope, and you can deny that at your peril or accept it and work on it. No happy arranged marriage surprises me: They get tossed in and told to work it out, which gives them better odds than the couples I see who think their issues will work themselves out because they purport to love each other. But that too is something you're going to figure out or not; the people I know who haven't learned it are maintaining a theory against evidence only a little less irrational than thinking the Earth is flat.

What happened sped up the process of discovering things about myself: some good, such as knowing I will find a way to survive after hitting bottom, and some bad, such as refusing to end a shitty relationship because I'm too invested in an illusion. I would like to think I learned a permanent lesson, but I did almost exactly the same thing ten years later. We illustrate discoveries that changed us in profound ways, yet we profoundly do not change.

DATING 101: COMEDY

I like short girls. I like tall girls too, but I like short girls more, probably because I feel more manly around them and don't have to stand up straight. I also like redheaded girls, not for any real reason, really just because I've never slept with a redhead, and I feel gypped about that. Most important, I like funny girls.

So when I get a message on a dating site from a four-foot-eleven redheaded stand-up comic, I can hardly believe my luck. We set up a date immediately, and she shows me some YouTube videos of her work, which include her in an improv comic singing group. Improv comedy is hard. Improv singing is hard. I have no idea how hard it is to make up four-part harmonies that are funny on the spot, but I imagine it's pretty hard. She's the real thing. She also has a pretty fabulous blog.

This is going to be fantastic, I think.

The First Problem

Remember that bit about short redheads? Well, as soon as I see her, I remember that part of that attraction comes from my relationship with my now long-dead ex-girlfriend Lauren, who was four foot eleven and had red hair. Most of the time, even around short redheads, this doesn't come up, but this girl looks almost exactly like her, which hadn't registered in the pictures I'd seen online. She even moved like her, which was probably the trigger.

So upon shaking her hand, I'm flooded with memories and suddenly questioning why I'm here and why I've been checking out short redheads all these years. Fortunately, I have the presence of mind to not open up the date with, "Wow, you look like my dead ex, and I am consumed with confusion and guilt," but that was just about all I could think about for the next four hours, even after drinking as much and as fast as I could (which wasn't much; see below). I should have gone home immediately, but my brain solves most confusion, guilt, and death issues by getting horny and trying to have sex with someone.

So the date went on.

The Second Problem

One of my friends works on radio shows with comedians, and he dropped this bit of wisdom about a year too late: "You know, I love comedy. Comedians, not so much."

This makes sense when you think about it. You know when you're out with your friends and you all start telling jokes, and everybody's laughing? You notice how hard it is to tell a really funny joke without laughing yourself, at least after the punch line? You know how if you see someone laughing it's hard not to laugh yourself? Comedians are people on a stage telling really funny jokes, and they're not laughing. Laughing is a hardwired form of human bonding, and comedians train themselves not to do it so they can make other people do it. They analyze people laughing and calibrate their routines to make people laugh at certain moments, and judge themselves on how effective they were at manipulating other people's bonding reflex.

In other words, comedians tend to be dark, antisocial, and weird.

My date was no exception. She didn't laugh. At all. Not once. She smiled exactly twice. It was like being on a date with a talking turtle. I realized I was working to entertain her, and she was off the clock, and had no interest in laughing or telling any jokes. When I didn't feel like she was examining me, I felt like she was wondering if I'd give her any material, and mostly thinking, *Nah, not much here.* The few times she told me something funny I had to laugh, because it was great, and she just stared at me, which made it funnier, but not the kind of funny you want on a date.

The Third Problem

She was a nonsmoking vegan lightweight.

I had to sneak cigarettes during bathroom breaks, which was probably futile, but I did it anyway. I couldn't really drink at the rate I wanted to, because people start to notice when you've had five whiskeys on ice and they're a third of the way through their first martini.

I'm not what you'd call a heavy drinker or a heavy smoker. I do both too much, but not in the way that's going to kill me before fifty or sixty. I don't wake up drunk, and I haven't thrown up from drinking in years. However, I do consume single cigarettes and beverages about twice as fast as most people. Since I was having almost as little fun as it's possible to have on a date with a guilt-inspiring ghost from my past, I really, really needed to drink and smoke, but had to do both at an inconspicuous rate, so every time I got a new drink, I'd finish it in about two minutes, then wait half an hour to get a new one. Since I wasn't smoking, I spent a lot of those intervening minutes trying to figure out what to do with my hands.

By the time veganism came up,* I knew this was a failed experiment. There was no way I could sustain this sham long enough to get her clothes off, although since quiet and weird girls tend to be freaks in bed, I was still sort of trying. But the thought of another long, emotionally confusing night of not smoking or drinking or eating meat was too much.

---

* Because taking eggs from chickens is still hurting the chicken. Clearly, my usual response, "Who really gives a fuck about a chicken?" was not going to go down well.

I bailed and let her walk to the subway herself. I would have been more gentlemanly, but I desperately wanted a cigarette and had to get to another bar.

Epilogue

Because I'm a fucking idiot, I did halfheartedly try to drum up another date a little while later. I wrote, "Hey, I had a pretty good time if you want to try that again." She replied, "Well, I guess I'm glad to have been a part of your pretty-good-time-having. I'll call you when I get back to the city."

She hasn't called.

ONLINE DATING

This isn't about the indignities I suffered at the hands of my former employers.[*] It's about the insights into the world of online dating and people in general that kept me hooked on the job long after I checked out on being a part of the actual work.

OkCupid is run by elitist math majors. I have no problem with math majors; I'm dating one. I have a huge problem with elitists. I have a problem with people who use the phrases "the average person" or "the man on the street" as synonyms for "people dumber than I am." I've always found it interesting how math and engineering majors deride philosophy majors, while philosophy majors dismiss math and science people, all with the same justification: Your discipline isn't hard enough. Ironically, the only people who give equal respect to all branches of the educational tree are the people who never climbed any of them.

---

[*] Apart from a few cheap shots.

The point is, they are math majors, they don't respect you, and they are calculating your sexual and romantic desires. This is not unique to OkCupid; all dating sites pay a bunch of programmers to run statistics on your messaging and activity habits to optimize their algorithms and interfaces to make money. This is the dark truth about Internet dating: A lot of people are paid a lot of money to commodify your need for companionship.

But this is not the dark truth many people sublingually hint at with the comment, "There's just something, I dunno, weird about it," and other dismissals of e-dating. The technophobic aversion to online dating usually has something to do with fears of seeming desperate, or the more amorphous fear of The Machine Taking Over Our Lives.* Online dating is just like bar dating: Attractive women are swarmed by creeps, intelligent people occasionally find one another, charismatic men get laid whenever they want, the awkward remain awkward, insincerity is punished, and sincerity is hit or miss. The oddest thing about most of these critiques of web-based trysts is that they fail to take into account the fact that the people involved still have to meet and like one another for anything exciting to happen, so ultimately, you're still dating the "normal way." You, as an individual, neither gain nor lose by taking your game online. If you want to say something about dating sites being creepy, use this:

---

* There is a machine doing that, but it's Facebook.

Working as a video editor for an infomercial production house taught me that people are systematically categorized in terms of fuckability and how much profit that fuckability can generate for products that don't work. This wasn't new to me; what was new was being one of the people doing the actual math. It was our job, literally, to confuse an audience's reason with calibrated sexuality; in an instant, a short lifetime of sensibility and empathy can be replaced by the quest for a firmer, whiter set of tits and an Asian woman who looks like a teenager. OkCupid taught me how to do this en masse. If editing for cleavage to sell Viagra rip-offs is a kind of murder, working at a dating site is a genocide. As dating sites collect data on users, they apply it back to the dating pool, and they hone in on the most attractive tier, advertising them to other users and the world to draw more traffic. This particular form of applied statistical analysis serves to entrench the social image of beauty and the most superficial stratification of biological and cultural lotteries. Like video production, it's an exploitation of greed and lust, but the method of commodification is the provision of the means for satisfying the public's desire for intimacy.

See? That's much creepier.

The core difference between dating online and off-line is the same as the difference between dating in Ellsworth, Maine, and dating in Manhattan: quantity of contact. Quality remains unchanged. Over the years of working for and patronizing dating sites, I've heard a number of people say "he/she uses X dating site and brings home all these disgusting men/women/creeps/tramps" which I don't doubt, but these people would be bringing home the same demographic were they using nondigital means.

A friend of mine dismisses dating sites on the grounds that it's too obvious that all the people want is sex. In my two decades of dating, I've been offered an unsolicited bathroom blow job from a stranger twice in a bar, and only once on the Internet.[*] People always want sex. For a set of attractive-enough or available-enough people, the Internet offers no more or less the opportunity of getting sex than the bar. I would even say that dating sites have a population more inclined toward meaningful, non-sex-based relationships than the average Saturday night crowd at the venue of your choice. Since the inception of online dating, one of the more common introductory lines has been "sick of the bar scene." This is usually a cry from women, who comprise the only gender that's usually sick of people pestering them for sex. I would never generalize to the point of saying there aren't members of both genders trolling the web for one-night stands, but the ratio of them to people looking for a more involved, or at least prolonged, relationship is isn't much different online than offline, and online it falls in favor of the prolonged. Women, and some men, go on dating sites to get a more thorough testing phase before committing to conversation, phone numbers, and bed. Consider that someone using a da-

---

[*] I declined all three, for safety reasons.

ting site can use a computer and read, and their writing skills are on display, as is their opinion of themselves. I can't figure out why people consider a face-to-face meeting a better indicator of character. It's a far better way to judge sexual charisma, but it's a terrible way to judge anyone with even a shred of self-awareness. Anyone who says they are a good judge of character in reference to people they've known less than one hundred cumulative hours is as self-delusional as people who say "I'm a people person" with a straight face, which is like saying "I'm a human being" as if it were an achievement. The speaker is either an idiot or a psychopath. Assuming a barely honest online self-description and a photo shoot, you have a handful of empirical data before you commit to spending time with someone.

This, however, is no guarantee. The following is a common exchange on dating sites:

From: Some_dudexxx
Subject: Hi there
You seem really nice, and cute. I saw you liked
DMB, I just saw them in concert. Interested
in a drink?

From: CuteChick293781
Subject: Re: Hi there

Hey, thank you! I'm not interested, but good luck! :)

From: Some_dudexxx
Subject: Re: Re: Hi there
well FUCK U U FUCKING STUK UP CUNT I DONT THINK UR THAT HOT ANYWAY WHORE

Yes, it sucks. But at least it only took three e-mails as opposed to three dates. There is rarely any evidence of this extremely common male behavior before it happens. In online dating, there is forewarning.

You can also get an inkling of a potential date's date-maturity level by understanding the evolution of the profile. After perusing thousands of profiles while bored at work, I've identified three distinct stages of profile design. The following isn't a strict progression, but profiles will in general proceed along these lines. Some exceptional profiles will skip to the end, and some will stagnate in the middle, but the important thing is you that should only contact people in the last stage.

The first stage is the joke profile. This encompasses several styles of profile writing, but they are all a joke in some sense or another. The most common form is "I just joined this site as a joke," also known as "My friends made me do it," or "This is so desperate, I can't believe I'm here." These profiles always do badly, unless the composer is an attractive young girl, in which case it doesn't matter what they write. Newcomers are always shy, and not admitting to what you're doing, or claiming you're doing it ironically, is the easiest way to peek over the diving board without jumping. There is a particular class of these profiles made up of girls seeking attention. Guys generally don't seek attention that won't theoretically lead to sexual satisfaction; some girls do. The attention-seeking subclass never moves past this initial stage.

The next most common variation in this stage is the Dadaist profile. Men and women write things like "I enjoy kicking babies" and their favorite things are porn, donkeys, and setting Barbie dolls on fire. These people are not crazy: Crazy people write social manifestos in their profiles. Like the "I don't know how I got here" people, the Dadaist profiles are exploring the site under the cover of irony by setting up as creepy and nonsensical a front as possible. Isn't that clever? This is a profile on a dating site and I'm trying to be unappealing and scare people away. Ha ha. Note that after the pictures of playing cards, dead animals, and historical atrocities, there is at least one full-body glamour shot.

Finally, there is the "I am a golden god" joke profile. They don't think it's a joke: These people have had all the luck the Irish could have hoped for had history been less of a bitch. They're looking for a queue of ladies and/or gentlemen so they can be sure they've vetted the human race sufficiently to choose an ego receptacle for a multiyear tenure without feeling shorted. These profiles are a tiresome list of achievements, judgments, and demands, and often include a pedigree. If you're like me, ignore these profiles. If you're like them, make it happen; you'll be content for multiple years.

The next stage is the self-deprecating stage. It cries, "See through my humility to my beautiful self." As alarming as this logic sounds, nobody is immune to the temptation to use this method of self-presentation. It's not a terrible thing, it's just what the unpopular kids did in high school,* and it's a defense mechanism. Since almost everyone in this abstracted social world goes through one of the joke-stage styles of profile design, they all feel the rejection the unpopular kids in high school felt, so they go through the self-deprecating stage that people who have been told they should be deprecated go through.

At last, if the user hasn't given up and is actually interested in getting a date, their profile will become a straightforward, honest presentation of themselves. At this point, they may still seem like jokers or self-deprecators, and you may not be able to tell they've reached the "This is actually me" stage. As a rule of thumb, if the profile is more than a year old and the person behind it is a reasonably regular visitor, this is as much insight as you're going to get.

So say you've found an honest-looking profile depicting an attractive and seemingly not crazy person. You write, and don't get a reply. You write to someone else. No reply. You conclude all profiles are fake.

---

* I know because I did it.

Don't feel bad; your questionable statistical analysis of two data points is not uncommon. To the numbers: Less than 5 percent of profiles are scams or cam whores.* The rest are legitimate, at least on OkCupid, which has more advanced methods of getting rid of fake profiles every day. Fake accounts are an onslaught nobody can stop, but most dating sites are making genuine efforts to keep it under control, and OkCupid tries harder than most because they don't advertise and rely on word of mouth and popular press. If you have a brilliant idea about how to stop people from creating fake profiles, rest assured that it's either been tried, or is currently in place.

However, many men just starting out online feel like everybody's fake for two reasons. First, they write a bunch of e-mails that consist of "hey cutie" and expect a response. Hint: If it doesn't work in a bar, it won't work on a dating site. In fact, having an opener that will lead to a conversation online is significantly harder than in person. People rarely dismiss you out of hand in person. Online, it happens all the time, partly because girls would rather not have "U FUCKIN WHORE" screamed at them when they reject someone, which is much less likely to happen in public than through e-mail. If

---

* *Cam whore* is a highly technical term for a forty-year-old man running online striptease sites, who creates fake profiles with pictures of models to entice subscribers.

you are consistently getting no replies, I suggest going to a bar and getting some feedback regarding your game.

The second reason guys get the feeling that all the girls are fake is that they persistently write to profiles containing nothing but a few pictures of a girl in her underwear, and a paragraph about liking sex and boys who play video games. This is a simple failure of logic on the part of the boys attempting correspondence. It is true that most girls wear underwear, and it is true that most boys play video games, so it is quite likely that there are girls who wear underwear who like boys who play video games. It does not follow that there is a horde of girls posting half-naked pictures of themselves on the Internet whose primary requirement for a mate is a penchant for *Call of Duty*. This comes back to the basic lesson of the Internet: The representation of the thing does not denote its physical existence. You should know that, and I have no sympathy for your disappointment if you don't.

At this point, you've probably noticed the widening gap between using a dating site as a female versus using it as a male. It's no different from the usual divide, however: men struggle with disappointment, women get harassed. Men spend their whole lives throwing themselves at women. The messages from men to women outnumber the competition five to one. Men are also more likely to send unsolicited pictures of their genitals. I'm assuming that somewhere, somewhen, a woman has sent an unwanted picture of her genitals to a man, which saves me the trouble of dividing over zero, so I can say the ratio is about a billion to one. Attractive women can barely read their mail, if they bother at all, as the torrent is intense, immediate, and mostly consists of the above-mentioned "hey cutie" e-mails, with a not insignificant smattering of "ur prtty."

One story should illustrate why this happens. Early during my employment, we deleted a man who had sent three hundred messages in one day, all of which were the same graphic description of him masturbating to the recipient's pictures. Two hundred and ninety of the women ignored him, nine told him to fuck off in so many words, and one wrote back, "Well sir, you certainly know how to turn a girl on. Kudos!! I look forward to more."

Dating is a numbers game. The bigger your numbers, the better the odds, and no matter who you are, you will eventually run across someone who wants you, and especially you, regardless of your height (if you're a man) or weight (woman) or how inscrutably awful your game is (idiot). Volume is the strength of all things interwebby. This strength carries the same risks as anything else provided in abundance, namely saturation and addiction. In rare moments of self-control, I've deleted my online dating account, for the same reason I've cut back drinking and hitting on people in bars; eventually, it feels like grazing or, to use a metaphor farther up the food chain, going to a cattle market. But I reject completely the notion that the Internet had anything to do with this depersonalization of intimacy. It comes from sleeping with too many people for too many terrible reasons, and just because the Internet offers other forms of depersonalization doesn't mean it's the Internet's fault that you can't remember the names of all the people you have to call after a shitty day at Planned Parenthood.

Dating sites are to dating as any other information technology is to the aspect of life it's meant to enhance: they increase efficiency.* People confuse their dreams of eternal romance with step one, which is meeting available mates. This is largely because people often secretly believe in love at first sight, fate, perfect couples, and all that other shit.† Dating sites make meeting other people more efficient. They serve no other purpose.

The vague claims they make are best ignored. eHarmony, aside from being evil, is a personality-matching machine for producing heterosexual Christian marriages. If you're not heterosexual or Christian, do you want to take a love test designed for those who are? My eHarmony account has recommended fifteen thirty-year-old single mothers, all of whom smoke and live in Pennsylvanian suburbs. This is clearly not the algorithm for me. OkCupid seems to do better

---

* Ideally, that is. I've never seen a code base that wasn't a map of pain with an X over a beast, the primary purpose of which is to consume man hours and hair pigment. Sometimes I think the future is here, sometimes I think it will never come.

† They must also believe in retroactive destiny caveats, because if you believe there really is one perfect mate out there, you should be scouring every dating site in the world to find them, so there must be a mechanism that undoes fate if you happen to meet said person online.

with its user-generated compatibility, but has a tragic flaw: Do you really want someone who's just like you? Do you even want someone who's everything you say you want?

There is one small advantage of a dating site over normal dating. The people who are most afraid of appearing desperate tend to be the ones who are desperate, and the people who dismiss everybody who isn't getting laid whenever they want as desperate are vapid. Neither of these types of people join dating websites, so you can instantly cut out a vast swath of annoying personalities.

DATING ADVICE FOR THE END OF CIVILIZATION

The end is probably nigh, and one should take this into consideration when entering a new romantic relationship. Since my expertise lies neither in combat nor science, I hope this small contribution to the far side of civilization as we know it will keep me from being immediately used for food or fuel.

The Crake Scenario

We've successfully used our technology to take ourselves out of the game.

This one is probably worst case. Somebody, somewhere, invented something targeting humans for the sake of, you know, stuff that made sense at the time. The most likely perpetrators are psychopaths and tree huggers. Doesn't matter. They made a virus or some tiny robots and effectively eliminated the human species.

   This presents obvious challenges for dating if there are any survivors at all. There probably won't be enough of a gene pool to repopulate the species, so babies will be more of a nuisance than anything else. Marriage will also be difficult, since if any priests make it through the near extinction, they will likely have to answer more questions than they can survive. There will be no government, so no judges, though you could probably find a ship captain somewhere.

The total collapse of any chance of a future will encourage a kind of despairing hedonism. If you're not equipped for this kind of lifestyle, I suggest a prompt suicide. Many people intent on filling up their dating history will find it filling up with domesticated livestock.

Good opening line: "We can either hang out or wander around with no one to talk to until we kill ourselves."

The Gore Theater

We didn't get our technology up to spec quickly enough to offset the effects of climate change, and we're all starving to death due to crop failures and no longer able to recover from weather-related natural disasters.

The most frustrating thing about this future is that even after the seas reclaim Florida, hurricanes become weekly events, and Jersey is a tropical paradise, there will be people *still* claiming that climate change is a hoax. On the bright side, we'll be able to shoot them at this point, but you should be prepared for the chance that you will have to have this conversation, again, during early courtship.

Here the species has certainly dwindled, but has a chance, so there's some cultural preservation, more a "We're all in this together" sensibility, and some prospect of hope absent from the Crake Scenario, plus a notion of repopulating. Monogamy will be under some strain in this, but many otherwise emotionally stagnant or unwise relationships will be artificially held together by false intimacy arising from constant shared struggle and danger. This will make fantastic literature for future generations, so it will behoove us to have them and pretend it was all worth it while we wait a thousand or more years for society to get back on its feet.

You'll want to go one of two routes with your relationship here. There's the isolationist, on-the-run style, which will guarantee a passionate relationship as long as you can sustain protein and vitamin levels, but your trip will be cut short eventually by bands of guerrillas and insane little cults.

A better bet is probably to find the largest available community, where numbers and common cause tend to smooth out the dangers. There will be a lot of griping about sex and relationships and protectiveness, but at least it will be griping and the occasional fatality instead of dozens of angry people with machine guns and a tenuous respect for the sanctity of life. Avoid communities relying on loose sheet metal for shelter, because again, lots of hurricanes, and that shit will cut through you like spinning metal through skin.

Good opening line: "I have food."

The Wachowski Gambit

We did get our technology up to spec, but we are now enslaved by our robot overlords.

Here things get tricky, because our interaction and breeding habits will no longer be up to us. Our skills will be relatively pointless for our silicon masters, as they will be able to do everything better than us, and anybody who thinks we have the remotest chance in a war against sentient machines doesn't understand technology.

The only real chance for humans in this scenario is that we'll be pets. This isn't so bad: We'll be bred and pampered, maybe even given books and toys with which to amuse ourselves. There will be illegal, underground human fights, we'll be bred for special characteristics and funny faces, and they'll have human shows where humans will solve calculus problems in stadiums and it will be adorable. We'll get the finest medical care until we get too expensive or old, then we'll be machinely put out of our misery.

The logical outcome of this is that, at least by human standards, we'll all be genius Olympic athletes and sex will be fantastic.

Good opening line: "They're closing the human park in twenty minutes, and come on, look at us. We're goddamn gorgeous."

The Kurzweil Leap

We are a godlike transhuman species.

The first two situations present the most difficult obstacle to overcome, namely nonexistence. The temporary nature of romantic struggles will be brought into sharp relief when the projected lifespan for all age groups drops to "tomorrow." The Kurzweil Leap presents the opposite difficulty, as the projected lifespan increases to forever, and you're not really human anymore.

In a transhuman society with unlimited lifespans, "till death do us part" will become an increasingly difficult promise to make, especially since the nature of physical form and identity will become a little cloudy when we're all nodes on the galaxy-spanning superintelligence. Alpha Centauri Sally may be a quiet, monogamous type focused on cataloging alien bacteria, while Sirius 9 Sally is a synthetic space frog seeding experimental sperm nebulas. You won't even be sure whom or what you're "dating" in the first place, and even if you've sorted that out, you can just spin up a few trillion virtual outcomes and see what sticks. Virtual and physical will be difficult to distinguish. We'll likely dispense with the notion of individuality, but there will be a middle stage where totally immersive virtual porn will involve creating people and sheep indistinguishable from the real thing and who will probably constitute conscious beings. This will bring up a host of ethical problems, which will hasten the process of dispensing with individuality.

What it even means to have children will be difficult to pin down. If Frog Sally releases a million Sallyish algorithms which mix with Reptile Phil's algorithms and incubate and recalculate in the solar winds of a dwarf star purporting to be the Accountant Formerly Known as Doug (who always just wanted to be a star), the resulting little Phil/Sally/Doug intelligences may be children, strictly speaking, but it's doubtful that even Doug will want to sort out whether they classify as dependents.

As postapocalyptic movies have taught us, things usually don't go well for women in tribal cultures that used to be entitlement cultures, or at least for women who lack the genetic predisposition to be Tina Turner. This, fortunately, won't be a problem in transhuman society, where we'll quickly forget what gender roles even mean.

All in all, we should probably shoot for this one.

Good opening line: Something really clever, probably in quantum Mandarin, Neptunian dialect.

FULL DISCLOSURE: ANXIETY

One of my oldest memories is of my dad running out of the house naked and screaming, then coming back in a few minutes later, looking sheepish. The neighbors had come out just in time to see him fly into a rosebush. Because of this memory and others like it, I can say I inherited my more dramatic panic attacks from him, and this is part of the explanation I have to give to anyone I share a bed with for more than a few months.

I call it the screaming attack, or the punch-the-wall attack. It crawls in quickly, but sometimes I can feel it coming; if I feel it early enough, I can deflect it in my mind and think about something else. A little later, I can punch a wall, and the pain resets my thoughts enough to move on. If I'm too late, I start screaming. It's always the same scream: "No, no, NO, NO!" and it terrifies anybody who hasn't heard it before. The panic is about death, which I always fear in the normal, abstract, death-is-bad sort of way, but I don't think about it or worry about it all the time. I can even intellectualize it as simply ceasing, and having had blackouts before, I know suddenly losing consciousness can be pleasant, since your ability to care or fear is one of the first things to go. The screaming happens most often in the morning, during the period where my brain is drifting around in pre- and semi-conscious states, when I've let loose a little of the control I try to keep on my thoughts the rest of the time. It used to happen right before I fell asleep, but I've perfected a combination of TV shows and alcohol to prevent evening attacks.

The fear isn't about what death is, or that it might happen soon. It's about viscerally knowing that it will happen. The inevitability that someday, no matter how hard I cling to life, no matter what I do, no matter what happens, some breath will be my last, and everything that I am will disintegrate forever. There's no place to run, nothing I can do. Some unmarked point in my future will make all my life past.

Aside from bruised knuckles and frightened lovers, this is a manageable anxiety. The second kind I suffer from is worse, and it's the one I have to explain to my employers every year. It started happening after my depression and social anxieties subsided, so it seems odd that after dealing with all that I would be rewarded with something even more functionally crippling.

I don't know what triggers it. It seems to start with health concerns, but, being a hypochondriac, I have those every day and have learned to ignore them and stop myself from looking up symptoms. But sometimes I can't ignore something, and I think I'm about to have a stroke, so I do my mental checkup: Multiplication, map visualization, logic problems, name of the president, count to ten, say the alphabet, track back my important memories as far as I can go, and list my errands for the day. This always comes up clean, but it doesn't help. I start wondering why it's not helping, and the anxiety starts building up, causing unfamiliar muscle twitches, the beginning of a headache (is this a stroke? Or an aneurysm? They say you can't feel an aneurysm, but what if you can feel the deadly ones right before they kill you? How would anyone know?), and increased heart rate (heart attack?).

I tell myself I've been through it before, but it doesn't help. If I'm at work I sit in the bathroom for twenty minutes, which buys me another hour in the office, but then the feedback between the white noise in my head and my body's alarm system starts breaking me apart. I shake uncontrollably and switch between thinking I'm dying and thinking I'm going insane. Sometimes I have enough time to tell my employer what's happening, sometimes I just make a quick apology and leave.

If my brain settles on dying, I make a doctor's appointment. If it settles on madness, I call a few friends who know why I'm so afraid of losing my mind. Either way, I rarely make it home. I go to a bar where no one knows me and start drinking, trying not to rub my head or scratch at myself too much. By the third drink, I'm okay, and embarrassed. I thank the bartender and call my doctor to apologize.

I'm useless for the rest of the day. I can't write, work, or focus: My body is exhausted and my brain is rebooting. If I pick up an instrument, I just play slow chords in minor keys, not caring enough about the next note to produce a melody. I try to stay around friends for a while, then I go home to watch TV, but can never decide on a show or a movie because none of them seem to be exactly the right thing to watch right then. The same thing happens when I look through my books. I end up playing video games and chain-smoking. I can't drink fast enough to get drunk, so I go to sleep staring at my cats, thinking about people to whom I never had the chance to say I was sorry.

On top of these two anxiety issues, anybody who is more than twenty minutes late to an appointment has died horribly, as far as my brain is concerned. And I don't just think, *Something must have happened,* no, I think, *Oh my God, my girlfriend was attacked by a five-foot-seven man with a knife and a baseball cap on a dark road four blocks from the subway and she's been raped and stabbed and is dying but I won't get to her in time and I won't get called by anyone until Monday and I'll spend the next month crying alone in my apartment until I lose my job and get evicted and end up drinking myself to death in my parents' living room just to make the nightmares stop.*

I think this anxiety has developed over the years, coddled by my OCD, as a result of my tendency to get exactly what I want accompanied by my ability to lose it in spectacular ways. While this cycle caused me to become existentially comfortable with the loss of anything except my life, the anxious, unwanted, nagging part of my brain is in a state of constant terror. Sometimes it's just saying, "You're gonna fuck it up, you're gonna fuck it up," until I say, "Fine! I'll fuck it up, just give me a goddamn minute," or I boot up *World of Warcraft*. The rest of the time it's saying, "The universe is going to take it away, the universe is going to take it away, you know it, it doesn't care about you and it will take away everything you care about." The problem with the second point is that I know it's true, and when it inevitably happens, my brain will get to say, "I told you so," and that will be an expensive week of drinking.

PRUDENT I SEX

I was flipping through Google News while waiting for a friend, and I came across the irresistible headline "Sexting is more common than you might think." It didn't really apply to me, as I assume the behavior is ubiquitous, so there's no way it could be more common than I think. It was the usual rigmarole about how shocking it might be that kids well into puberty are experimenting with sexual communication. One of the related articles brought up the statistic that "Those who have been the victim of digital abuse are more likely to be sexually active or to have engaged in 'risky' behavior, such as stealing, using illegal drugs, drinking alcohol, or smoking."

The conflation of sex, drugs, alcohol, stealing, and sending dirty pictures is the closing argument for denying puritans the right to publish, and in general for keeping statistics out of the hands of people who exploit the general public's inability to distinguish between correlation and causation. The perfunctory *or* and the quotes around *risky* do not excuse the author's phrasing.

But after my standard gut reaction,* I read a marginally better article that focused on suicides ostensibly motivated by naked pictures being forwarded to friends and not-so-friends. The first, worse article, reported "12 percent of those who engaged in sexting activity have contemplated suicide." Considering psychiatryonline.org puts the proportion of teens contemplating suicide at 19 percent, these kids are doing pretty well. I'm curious how these studies phrase their inquiries; technically, I'm contemplating suicide right now, and have many times in the past, without the vaguest inclination to actually do it. Also, two suicides resulting from some pandemic form of digital abuse or public humiliation sort of makes me want to get up and applaud what is obviously the safest risky behavior in town. These are outliers, like most sensationalized suicides.

Though these articles are bright and shining examples of how to distort an issue without actually saying anything false, they put me in mind of the many e-mails I received while at OkCupid, sent by people who screamed at us for not protecting the pictures of themselves they put online to attract mates. Since most people have Windows PCs, and most Windows PC keyboards have a "Print Screen" button, it's tempting to write back to these people to point out that they're using a service designed to let people post pictures for a global audience, for free, and it's a little odd to get upset

---

* Namely, "Deal with it."

that somebody saw it and was able to copy it because it's a piece of digital information and the immense ease of replicating and transmitting digital information is a legacy issue that arose from the fact that THAT'S WHY WE INVENTED THE TECHNOLOGY IN THE FIRST PLACE you fucking idiots.

In my younger days, I didn't know the difference between "reply" and "reply all," and that resulted in me sending my social security number to five hundred strangers, several people who didn't like me, and at least one person who liked me way too much. Older and wiser, I now know that this was a particularly bad example of the standard "reply all fail," and it is very important to check who is included in the send-to box of any email. The point is that people don't recognize how quickly and destructively their information can be made available to millions of people by accident, to say nothing of a motivated adversary.

This kind of technological ignorance, which is thankfully waning in the first-world public, is not their primary problem. It's their inability to grasp that the heavily advertised "connectivity and sharing" is exactly the same thing as the much feared "vulnerability and exposure" that results from information being an increasingly communal commodity. This misunderstanding of how information works and travels is shamelessly hijacked by those trying to convince us that all sex is a form of abuse by writing articles about how blooming sexuality leads to humiliation and death. The irony is that the people writing these articles seem unaware that the libido is not going away, and the constant juxtaposition of abuse and death with sex is just laying the psychological groundwork for that really twisted porn that makes normal people not want to have sex. On second thought, maybe it's not ironic at all, but I'd still rather dispense with both snuff films and the Christian Right.

I have a huge advantage in this world, which is the advice my dad gave me when I was ten years old: "Don't do anything you don't want on the front page of the newspaper the next morning." I admit that I interpreted that advice to mean stay under the radar and dispense with shame, but regardless of the moral implications of my decisions, they led to the gut instincts that prevent me from publicly screwing myself in the modern world of front pages for everyone.

Regardless of your level of shame or what you're willing to admit to, don't make a digital copy of anything you don't want to go public, or at least don't send it to anyone, or at the very least, be prepared to deal with it when the person you sent it to sends it to your teacher, your spouse, and your mother. That's it. I'm prepared to deal with every recorded piece of information about me being made public. You should be too, and that's what you should be teaching your kids, not telling them, and certainly not believing, that "sexting" leads to drug use and suicide.

WHAT IS AND WHAT SHOULD NEVER BE

I say a lot of stupid things.[*]

I don't mind being factually wrong, or discovering my logic is flawed. I've been wrong about a lot, and if someone points it out, I learn something. I've held strong opinions for years and discarded them because I decided they were naive or stupid. Sometimes I go a little too far with what I think is funny and my girlfriend doesn't talk to me for the rest of the day. I feel bad, but my intent is never to hurt.

The stupid things I say that bother me are the things I say because I'm blind to messages being put in my head by my culture. Things I would claim not to believe if pressed, but that sneak into my comments when I think I'm being cute, and I have to think, *Shit, do I believe that? Do I think that when I look around me?*

There are exactly two things I've permanently taken off the Internet after posting them.[†] One was a screed against two

[*] No, really.
[†] Not including the map to my apartment I took down after publishing my first book, when a fair number of people wrote to me asking me to

girls who had the indecency not to have sex with me at the same time. This isn't quite as offensive as it sounds: I in no way believed they were required to have sex with me, and I offered to drive them home after the sudden awkward moment that ended the evening. I was upset in that I wasn't even pursuing them at the time; one of the girls had set it all up in the hopes that her girlfriend would get back into their relationship if I was included in their sex life. An older, marginally more mature me would have seen the problems with this idea, and would certainly not have written a long public message to the tune of "please keep me out of your crazy" just because there wasn't a cold enough shower on the planet to make me forget I'd just gone from "about to have a threesome" to "watching public access alone in Maine on Tuesday in the middle of winter." I was chastised by my friends, and then hate-stalked by one of the girls for calling her crazy. She actually caught up to me at a mutual friend's apartment, and I had to hide in a roommate's room for the next two hours while I listened to her threaten to kill me, break my legs, and cut my balls off, in varying order. This worked out for me: The roommate came home and we got silently stoned in her room, trying to keep from laughing as we had a conversation on a legal pad about how this girl was crazy. Not crazy in the

---

hook them up with drugs. It suggested poor reading comprehension on their part, and I didn't want people with poor reading comprehension taking drugs and trying to find me.

sense of accusing girls of being crazy because it's easier than admitting you were a terrible boyfriend; crazy in the sense of severe bipolar disorder and multiple incidents of stalking former girlfriends.

Anyway. That was an insensitive thing to contribute to the situation, and I took it down. The other, in my mind, was significantly worse.

After getting into *Lost* and following it for its last three agonizing years, I watched the final four episodes in a late-night marathon, and got to the end at two in the morning on a weekend. I was so pissed off I went straight to the local bar and ranted for half an hour with the frothing vitriol you'd expect from someone who's just found out the man who murdered his sister went free because the arresting officers forgot to read him his rights.

In addition, I wrote this on Facebook: "J. J. Abrams, you are an incompetent fucking hack and you deserve to be raped like the drunk sorority girl that you are."

My mom pointed out to me what this sentence implied, and I then made a few lame excuses and took it down. A couple of hours later it hit me just how horrible a thing this was to say, and realized, on some level, I didn't have a lot of sympathy for sorority girls who went to frat parties and got raped, because that's what frat boys are like.

It does not excuse my behavior to bring up how my experiences with frat boys at large universities led me to believe anyone who even tries to join a fraternity should be under house arrest at all times. I have no problem with my history of advising girl friends to avoid certain frats because they're full of rapists. But that's not what I said on Facebook. I said, if you're a drunk girl in the Greek system, and you get raped, you deserve it. I was blithely supporting the rape culture I claim to hate.

Frat and sorority culture in general was such an alien world to me, I never bothered to think about how fucked up certain assumptions about it were, and even if those close to me never deserved to be raped, I allowed issues and alienations in my head to come to the conclusion that some girls deserve to be raped because they make bad decisions, because there's enough stupid in our society for an individual to silently hold that conclusion without being called out on it. More succinctly, I was blind to my privilege.

Luckily, I did get called out on it, and managed to stamp out one more hideous part of my personality, and started looking harder at the gender debates of our day. The first thing I discovered is how agonizing it is to try to keep on top of cultural dialogues in this idiot country. People who think the world was created seven thousand years ago scream that men are genetically predisposed to rape and dominance without ever noticing the incompatibility of those views, and are shouted down by people who say the mere act of talking to a strange woman is grounds for castration.

A lot of it seems like a debate between people who say they're not responsible for the way they are and people who say you are only the way you are because of some cultural assumption. There's a lack of voices saying yes, people have certain things built into them by culture and genetics, and it's their responsibility to suppress the darker parts.

I was a late bloomer in everything in which you can bloom late.* Among them, liking boobs. I liked girls for ages, but boob appreciation hit me all at once while I was talking to an ex-girlfriend at Dunkin' Donuts. I think I was nineteen, and while we were talking, I glanced down at her cleavage about six hundred times, and when I finally caught myself doing it, the conversation went something like this:

"So, I'm sorry, I keep looking at your tits."

"I noticed that! You didn't used to do that."

"I know, it's weird. I've never been a boob guy."

"Aww, you're becoming a man. It's going to make girls uncomfortable, just so you know."

That was the end of it between us. Since it does make girls uncomfortable, I try not to do it, especially when I'm talking to them. Do I want to stare at boobs all day? Of course. Is it rude to focus my attention on what I find sexually appealing when someone is talking to me? Of course. Should I whip myself for wanting to look at boobs? No. I'm

---

* Except math. I was gifted in math from age six until fifteen. I taught myself everything up to beginning calculus just because the books were lying around, and my reward from the public education system was teachers being frustrated because they had nothing to teach me for three hours a week. I was literally scolded for getting ahead of the class. I gave up in high school and phoned it in until I dropped out, and avoided math until I had to start doing it again to keep software jobs.

sexually attracted to women, and that attraction is the sum total of most of my thought processes. Should I excuse staring at boobs instead of faces because that's just the way I am? Of course not.

Arguing against this simple social nicety, or excusing it, is part of what lets rape culture keep its foot in the door, especially among people who claim to be on the right side. I'm attracted to women! Of course I'll look at them and be attracted. And if she's attractive enough and won't have sex with me, duh, rape. Meanwhile, our public shaming culture seems happy to demand women put out while condemning them for doing exactly that, and you don't have to lean far over the railing to see masses of people condemning all sexuality, which means we're not even starting at respect women and let gay people get married. We're not even at the point where we can let heterosexual couples who respect one another have consensual sex in peace. I don't only blame religion for this: it's softwired into young brains, and I recall multiple atheist high-school peers calling some women sluts and others ice queens in the same conversation. Within the shame culture, we have implicitly reserved the right to declare fault in all women who don't have sex with our preferred people on our preferred schedule.

There's a lot of sensible advice out there for how to teach men to respect women, but this alone is not enough. People need to be taught that just because they want something doesn't mean they're going to get it, or that it's acceptable to keep trying. We also need to look at the things we say for attention and see if they're indicative of destructive beliefs we're helping to propagate. And, though I deserved to be publicly smacked down for my behavior, we should not lose our sense of humor when dealing with these problems, because inspiring self-examination always does more good than overcondemnation or denouncement. If we lose our sense of humor, the dialogue descends into screaming lunacy, and that doesn't help anyone.

SABBATH AND CORAL

The *Maxim* magazines that have been showing up in my mailbox for the last four or five years are addressed to me, so I must have had direct involvement in whatever event initiated their continuing arrivals. Since we live in the age of post-scarcity as far as titillating ourselves is concerned, I doubt the thought *I sure could use a soft-core tease magazine a couple of steps below the Swimsuit Issue* crossed my mind, so I have no idea what that event was.

Reading a *Maxim* is a simple business: skim through, read some bullet points for either bad advice or occasionally funny misogyny, see if they finally slipped in something resembling a nipple, read the interview if you actually care, bathing suit, bathing suit, close the magazine and decide if it's aroused you enough to load up pornhub.com, annnnd . . . no, probably not. However, one issue, a few months ago, announced on the cover an article called "Dungeons and Dragons with Porn Stars."

Well, I thought, *those are things that I like.* The article was about Zak Sabbath, who runs a blog where he recounts bloggy-type things and D&D sessions with his fellow porn stars.

He also spells his name similarly to my mother's best friend's son, which seemed like an odd coincidence until I saw the picture in the article and fuck me it's the same person.

This is not the oddest thing that has happened to me over the years, but it was one of those rare discoveries that left me with absolutely no cues about how to react.

The last time I saw Zak, he was an artist of minor repute living not far from me in Brooklyn. We hadn't seen each other in years, and weren't exactly friends, but I was new to the city, and he was nice enough to grab coffee with me.

I think I was twenty-four at the time, still wandering around with deer eyes and thinking the city was just, gosh, just the swellest thing ever in the whole world. I still feel this way, but I have less energy and have learned to hide it around Europeans and people in scenes, because they both have that annoying reaction of "Oh my, are you still *excited* about life?" Zak was somewhere in the orbital swing around thirty, and seemed friendly enough but existentially unenthused, sort of like a European. I don't remember much of what we talked about, except for this exchange:

Me: "Yeah, looks like I'm becoming a programmer. Or at least spending too much time in front of a computer."

Zak: "Way too much of that these days."

He said it in this manner that seemed condescending and judgmental, and probably was, but it wasn't dissimilar from the way I say some things these days. I'm just more enthusiastic. The only other thing that stuck in my head was this, dropped at the end of the conversation, after we'd been chatting about my recent, unpleasant breakup with the girl who'd come to the city with me:

"I think men want to *do* something, while women want to *be* something."

I thought about that for longer than I care to admit. When you listen to someone while you're tuned to respect-fulness, ambiguous sentences with simple verbs and two clauses have more impact than they should. Any statement that brings up something like this makes you shuffle your memories looking for examples and counterexamples, and eventually you have sort out how you feel about men and women and how you interpret the words *be* and *do* in the first place. Though it may inspire useful reflection, you must eventually conclude that the original sentence meant absolutely nothing, then you start wondering where it came from and why anyone would say it, then you finally realize you don't care, ideally before you get to the second paragraph.

Even though I just spent a lot of words insinuating he was an asshole, Zak seemed cool and was definitely a lot hipper than I was, so we parted ways and I didn't really expect to see him again. Especially not in the back of a *Maxim*.

My first reaction was a kind of surprised, "Well, good for Zak," tempered by the fact that this isn't really how you want to come across people who used to beat you up when you were a kid. Zak was a default babysitter for me and my broth-er while my family was living in Pennsylvania, and he was terrible at it. He was a nasty, narcissistic little brat who yelled at us and wrestled us to the ground for fun since he was twice our size, while saying, "You think you'll summon your Hulk strength, dontcha? Not gonna happen." He grew out of it, and most little kids are obnoxious brats, so I don't hold it against him, but I sort of hoped some kind of uppance would come around for him. Instead, I find out he didn't even have to give up Dungeons & Dragons to get All the Sex. I would tell fate to go fuck itself, but I guess it's busy blowing Zak.

Those brief thoughts aside, it was time to tell everyone I knew that holy shit my old babysitter is a porn star, to which they all eagerly replied, no kidding what's her name? to which I replied, no it's a dude, to which they said oh, and lost interest. It's news for about half a standard bar cycle.

I didn't think much more of it until I got an e-mail from the aforementioned girl I moved to the city with, which said, among other things, "I'm making porn and suing the company I make porn for, haha."

This brought up some more complicated reactions.

My girlfriend recently asked me why I was so obsessed with the discovery that I had friends in the porn industry. The obvious motivation for this question and the obvious answer don't apply to our relationship, so I had to figure out something else. My response was that as a person who left the film industry a decade ago and has no contacts even remotely close to porn, I didn't expect to find two people from my personal life making it in the space of a month, and I didn't expect one of them to be an ex-girlfriend.

My relationship with Coral Aorta was odd and ended badly. We had an age gap that I will describe as "legal" and "very much on the edge of social acceptability in modern North American society." In retrospect, it was a perfect combination of my high school issues and her daddy issues, and marinated in the artificial excitement produced by our hesitance to admit the existence of our relationship to anybody. We happily met in secret for eighteen months, until circumstances dictated that we had to come out to everyone and I had to sit through a conversation that actually included the phrase, "What are your intentions with my daughter?"

Out in the open, we steadily cooled toward each other, since the age gap wasn't as easy to ignore when we were sharing social situations. Still, we futzed our way through it, and had a delightfully romantic parting. Then, both of us being a little overconfident, she moved to New York with me.

I later found among the things she left behind a rough sketch of me sporting a pig's head. I'm not sure which conversation prompted that, but it's safe to say that the desires of a young gypsy bisexual girl in New York City for the first time don't mix well with the desires of a mid-twenties programmer trying to get a foothold in his career. My first inkling of this was when she joined the Gay Pride Parade while Jake and I found a pool hall and got a solid afternoon buzz going. We were supposed to find her at Washington Square Park at the end of the parade, so we groggily made our way down and started looking around. I was a bit concerned about finding her until Jake said, "Oh my God," and I turned to follow his gaze—and everyone else's—to see Coral, topless in the fountain.

This was before I got over most of my jealousy issues, but I'm proud to say I wasn't really jealous at that point, just getting an impression that things weren't going to work out. She was just starting her adventures, and I was trying to forget mine. We met in the middle well enough, but were rapidly parting ways.

I knew it at the Dresden Dolls show, which is why this whole awkward summer never should have happened. This was the show where the brigade was in full swing, and the power went out for several hours, leaving it and me to mob the streets, juggle, and eventually blow fire in a very surprised stretch of Boston. I'm told you can find me somewhere on a Dresden Dolls DVD during all of this, but I haven't looked. I was hunched in too much of a suit, trying not to run out of cigarettes; Coral was letting strangers paint her next-to-naked body. It was clear I wasn't going to keep up.

Nearly a decade later, I still wouldn't be able to keep up. Hell, a couple of Facebook messages and I have to start thinking about how I feel about porn.

The exact feeling upon hearing the news of her porn career was sort of a null ennui. I wasn't really surprised, regretful, excited, sorry, or happy. Somewhere between a mild "wtf" and a committed "meh." I wasn't sure what I was reacting to, and I was in no position to judge, even if I'd had the inclination. Then I felt proud of my automatic nonjudgmental pseudoreaction, then wondered why I should deserve to feel weird about it, then knew, for a fact, that I had no desire to see her at work, then wondered about that, then wondered, most importantly, why I hadn't had anything like this reaction to Zak.

Obviously, gender. I could write a few paragraphs about how it's emotional blah or ex-relationship blah or closeness or recentness, and it would all be lies. I've been over our relationship for years, and knew a very long time ago she was going to have sex with a bunch of people immediately upon leaving my apartment. It wasn't my business then, and it's not my business now. Even more disturbing, I realized I had even less desire to see Zak's work than Coral's, which translates directly to me wanting to avoid seeing the penis of someone I know *more* than I want to avoid seeing a roomful of strangers gangbang my ex-girlfriend and current friend.

Since I pride myself on being progressive, egalitarian, and emotionally mature, this was a disturbing thing to have to admit to myself. Being 100 percent straight doesn't excuse this odd aversion to dick, nor the subtle distinction in my mind between what Coral and Zak are doing. Sure, there are far more sexually adventurous people than me who don't think about this, and far less progressive people who are already calling me a fag and burning this book, but I'm supposed to be one of the good guys, dammit.

What would Jon Stewart do?

I hope he would boot up Netflix on his PlayStation and watch *After Porn Ends*, because that's what I did. I needed to get a cultural reference point that didn't include pop-up windows.

The movie consists or interviews with former porn stars and a few people who study porn. The men are pretty blasé about the whole thing. The women range between laughing it off and joining antiporn causes.

Since all of my porn comes from the infinite tap dispensing amateur and pseudoamateur clips provided by the interwebs, I was surprised to see people I recognized. It's not really a surprise to find out they're thoughtful, normal people, but it's jarring since the entire genre is designed to prevent you from seeing them as that, from the bad camerawork to the ridiculous situations and bad dialogue. Umberto Eco referred to it as the "necessary artlessness of porn" and I wasn't completely sure what he meant until I saw a porn with high production values. It was off-putting. I kept paying attention to the lighting and wondering where the actors' parents were.

It clearly affected all of them internally. For some it was traumatizing; for others, it was just a past career. Externally, they were permanently judged by the very people who doubtlessly consumed their services; one of the porn scholars clearly could not separate the voices in his head, so he wrote an academic book on porn and explicitly referred to the actresses as whores. Internally, the ex-porn stars' reactions to these judgments were dictated by their self-judgment. Some didn't care; others were ashamed. All of them had to deal with their career's effect on their attempts to find work afterward: Getting a job in a conservative real estate firm was harder, postporn, than becoming a bounty hunter. Politician fell somewhere in between, but that was a weird year even for California.

So it wasn't much help to my situation, but I was impressed, as I rarely am by aspects of this country, how some of them could find social lives for whatever their postporn attitudes were. There's still a happy variety of subcultures hiding behind the intolerant common denominator we put on television.

The question, for me, returns to the experience of routine. A modern-day porn consumer has to be careful with their habits. It is true that you get desensitized, but this is not an endless cycle. It's not hard to take a break and get your imagination back up to speed. Like most gateway arguments, it's a lie that watching porn creates an inevitable descent into the weird and illegal because nothing else gets you off. The nature of the problem is just clicking around for that perfect clip in feverish arousal and accidentally clicking to something just over the edge of what you find acceptable; your brain makes a tiny little connection and you can't look at spatulas in quite the same way. You just have to decide where your limit is and what keywords are associated with things beyond that limit. "Zak" and "Coral," for instance.

And maybe that's the problem. I consume porn and masturbate in secret, carefully disposing of evidence. Most people do it, or suffer horribly because they don't do it, and among my people, everybody's ready to admit this as long they're never caught. If you break it down, it makes absolutely no sense that you'd be afraid of being caught masturbating by the person you have sex with on a regular basis, yet we're more afraid of being caught by them than anyone else. Porn capitalizes on this sexual shame, creating ludicrous scenarios often populated with bad people, everybody getting off on betrayal and abuse as much as they are on the actual sex, which is part of the reason porn loses its glamour so suddenly once you're done with it. Despite knowing this is all acting, and most of the people are having fun with it,* there's an active exploitation of *my* problems with sexuality, and that's not something I want to be personal. If I can use it and pretend it never happened, it's fine. But now that my friends are in it, I don't get to toss out the issues out with the tissues.† I have to admit I'm programmed to be ashamed of something I consider straightforward and natural, and I get off on that shame. And that's weird.

Fortunately, as with most people, there's a solid compartmentalization between porn and my real sex life, but why should that be? I know couples who watch porn together and that seems altogether healthier, but that's not going to work with everyone because not everyone likes porn. However you approach it, what's wrong is not with the fact that there's porn or the fact that people jack or jill off to it. What's wrong is the culture of being afraid of sex in general, which informs all ends of the sex industry from reading a *Playboy* to sex slavery.

---

* At least ostensibly in the porn I watch.
† Ever start writing a sentence that you just couldn't stop?

So, comfortable as I am with my run-of-the-mill porn, all my nonreactions amounted to not wanting to face the de facto discomfort built into my sex life and my relationship with masturbation. I resent it, and I'm not sure what to do about it, but I appreciate that people who lack this discomfort, or at least approach it differently, have made me look at it in a new way. Also, I'm totally not going to stop watching porn.

NOTCHES

It happens less and less frequently, but I still occasionally get into a conversation about how many people the participants have had sex with. I generally demure, unless it's important.[*] All of my answers are a lie.

It's not because I mean to lie. It's because I honestly don't know, and don't feel like getting into it. It's definitely more than fifty, probably hovering around sixty or seventy. Every time I try to work it out exactly, I find myself forgetting people, adding people twice under real name and nickname, and combining people into the same memory. Worse, when trying to make an official list, I discover my sexual history is riddled with difficult technical questions. What if there was penetration, but nobody got off? This could just be bad sex, but what about the flip side where there's no penetration, but everybody got off? What if there's no touching and one person got off? What if there was a lot of heavy petting and six gay men on the other bed? Or four lesbians on the couch?

[*] Important meaning stating a number will increase the chances of it going up.

Growing up during the Clinton presidency made these questions important, and even if they've been answered legally, what matters is the line after which you have to explain yourself, and that's a gray area. I often count the people with whom there was no outright missionary sex, but multiple make-outs with a chance of orgasm, but I exclude people with whom there was only one such session. Also, if someone goes down on me, that tends to count in other people's eyes, but if I go down on someone, people call it a loss. I have no explanation for this, especially since I tend to prefer the latter. Also interesting is that a threesome counts as two (or three, depending on the scoring system), even if one of the participants is playing a purely supportive role, even me.

With these technical concerns and a worsening memory, I do not know how many people I've had sex with. What I do know is that it's a weird number.

People like me tend to be in the twenty to thirty range. By people like me I mean straight, moderately attractive nonswingers. Our number usually hits thirty if we get to our late twenties without a wedding ring. And that's an open-minded—or at least horny—straight, moderately attractive nonswinger. Thirty bedmates provides enough experience to write a blues song and hold your own in the conversations that happen in single-sex company after five drinks. Swingers, experimental bisexuals, and people who want more sex than a single partner can provide have much, much higher numbers, at least three digits. It's usually not rock star level (which is at least four figures, or at least defies any attempt to make a list), but it's a lifestyle of sex, and far more than the average person.

So I'm well below the sex-person average, yet twice the norm for my demographic. Since I tend not to like the swingers, to whom I am essentially a virgin, and since the sexual norm considers me a slut, I avoid the sex-number conversation.

I also avoid it because the number changes connotations as it increases. Zero is at once pathetic and amazing after you're twenty, unless you're Catholic or similarly disabled. In early college two or three is acceptable, and that number should increase by two or three each year, on average. This college stage is when you start talking numbers if you're a guy, in friendly if passive-aggressive competition. Lying is expected within reason, and extensive description of sexual encounters is appreciated, though doubted.

I'm not sure when my number hit the slut* bracket, but I do know people with higher and lower numbers escape the slut designation. I myself hear it less and less since my current relationship passed the two-year mark. So number, although it's the only hard data point, does not alone a slut make.

Being a local anomaly helps. Being a couple of standard deviations from the expected average promiscuity in your

---

* I'm using *slut* as a catchall term for player, man-whore, skank, etc.; any derogatory-esque term for someone who likes having sex in excess of peer expectations.

demographic will raise eyebrows. I'd argue this just preps the package for slut labeling: It's hard to argue someone is a slut if that someone has slept with about the same number of people as everyone else in their social group.

Gender of course plays a role. *Slut* apparently originated as a term to refer to a woman of subpar personal hygiene, and could actually be applied to men, but, since men pretty much rule the world of social dialogue and didn't want to be called sluts, it became associated primarily with sexually promiscuous women. I suppose in the transitional period it was synonymous with *skank,* or *dirty slut.*

I'd like to attribute the fact that I've been called a slut by many people to social progress and the cooling of gender wars, but the fact remains, I'm not offended by it. Despite my clumping various terms of promiscuity into the single word *slut, man-whore* is probably the best—or only—way to add some implied offense to describing a sexually promiscuous man. Calling a guy a slut gets you a slap on the back, while calling a girl a slut gets you a slap in the face. There's been some reclaiming of the term, largely by the "ethical slut" contingent, but derogatory use when referring to a woman is still prevalent.

Though I'm not going to end up on the progressive side of the war over adding *ze* to the dictionary as a gender neutral pronoun,* I should point out that identifying as queer renders

---

* Mostly because it vould make it harder to make fun of ze Germans.

a person pretty much immune to socially derogatory terminology, because the queer community did such a good job of asserting a private terminology, and because when the conservative and naive communities hear *queer,* assuming they have any idea what it means, they hear *hell-bound gay slut* and try to shut it out. When I was growing up, queer was just a derogatory term for gay, and I applaud the fact that the sexually ambiguous, fluid, and nonstandard community took back the word so completely.

Regardless, just because the word *slut* has slipped across genders and can be applied to me doesn't mean there isn't a negative connotation to it. Mostly because of the attitude of the slut in question.

When I was dating three people at once, I was never referred to as a slut. I was being honest with them, and all of them came to hang out with my friends at various times. The slut times were when I was having sex early and often with a string of women, usually right after a breakup, as part of a mixed assault on my depression, supplementing alcohol and crying. I was using the act of getting sex to make myself feel better. Even the actual having of the sex wasn't as important as this subsistence-level acting out, trying to convince myself I was still holding up my end of some imaginary bargain with life. Not that I was admitting to any of that, since admitting it would defeat the purpose, and at the time it felt like more fun to pull out my iPhone and say, "Hey guys, guys, check out this hot chick I banged."

The excuse for this kind of behavior is not having had enough sex or mature, intimate relationships in my youth. It's not a great excuse, but it's the same one most people in this position have. It's compounded by being in an environment where you were supposed to have lots of sex, at least as a boy. Some people just have fewer urges or urges directed elsewhere, or some freakish happy relationship in their early twenties. Not me. I was supposed to have had more sex, and denying that I wanted it just made my relationships with women weird and awkward. Emphatically admitting it and then attempting to have more sex made everything much easier.

This, by the way, is how you graduate from being the "nice guy" that's not really nice, just hard up and bitter about his obsequious and dishonest nonadvances being rebuffed, to being able to approach at least moderately healthy sexual relationships without turning into a jackass who reads pickup-artist manuals. The most recent one I've seen traversing the gauntlet of Internet disgust has a whole section on "physical escalation," which is basically a guide on how to feel up women whether they want it or not until they sleep with you. The author does a bunch of backpedalling about how to backpedal when she tells you to fuck off, which shrieks manipulative date rapist. I wanted to tell him how physical pressure can frighten a girl enough to sleep with him because she's afraid he'll rape her anyway, but I doubted the conversation would go well. The fact is, whatever my motivations, when I met someone I wanted to have sex with, I did, and never used a pickup line in my life. Sex is a natural result of mutual attraction, or even mutual boredom, and you don't have to study guides on how to win the game if you just quit and treat people like people. That is the sole realization that changed my number from the single digit prior to twenty-two to the unknown quantity it is today, racked up in the few months here and there between monogamous relationships. So you can throw away all your manuals for mastering The Game: If you stop playing, you discover there is no game.

Of course, none of this means I wasn't trying to prove something to myself. That I could be attractive, that I could be desired, that I could be normal like the people in soda commercials. After dispensing with my awkwardness and self-doubt, I was in a haze of intimacy and sex. I was addicted to meeting people, to the sudden evaporation of nervous anticipation on the first date, to first kisses and navigating the city by coin flips. Desperation slipped away to reveal addiction.

Then, one day, I realized I'd slept with enough people. Enough, in my case, meaning I left my peers in the dust without meaning to, and could no longer remember exactly how many people constituted enough, who those people were, and what enough even meant. I had to stop and wonder why, and realize all the above things about social problems and feelings of inadequacy and substituting fake intimacy for sorting my shit out. Mercifully, I managed to pull all this off without acquiring an STD or too many enemies.

Something was lost. I remember when sex was always special and amazing, and it won't be again. The price for having all the kinds of sex you want in excess is a default disconnect between the act and whatever emotions led up to it. It's not that sex has lost any of its allure, but it's not a uniquely special thing in and of itself. It's arguable, and I've argued, that that's good, as we imbue sex with social superpowers because Western culture is so terminally afraid of it. But I do remember the wonder of it. The charged moments of wanting nothing so much as to touch one more inch of skin, in a long path leading over the edge of selfishness into the ecstasy of being lost in the arms of another person. That still happens, but not automatically, and not as a new experience.

Then again, that could just be my age talking. I'll never know.

NOBODY'S BITCH

Recently, my dear friend Gil told me that she hated the lead female character in my novel so much she almost stopped reading. If my book were actually published and sitting comfortably near the top of *New York Times* Best Seller List, I would have simply ignored her text and gone back to snorting cocaine off my hooker, but since Gil is one of the people I begged to help me edit the latest draft, I pushed the hooker off the bed* and investigated further.

My first reaction was that if I can create a character that inspires so much loathing that the reader becomes upset, go me. The character in question is a total bitch, rude and obnoxious to the very people cutting her breaks at every turn. She's also pretty, which is how people often get away with being like that. You're not supposed to like her in the beginning, and she's composed of elements of my girlfriends past and imagined, both good and bad. The root of my disagreement with Gil is that she sees the character as a bad person,

---

* She was dead anyway.

and I see her as a damaged person. More important, she thinks that a person can be damaged and still be bad, while I don't think anyone's bad. I think mean, vicious, and bitchy people are damaged and unhappy, and deserve some empathy, or in the worst cases, pity.

This discussion led to her next question: "Is there anybody you don't like?"

This gave me pause. This question and the implications of my answer pertain to the entirety of my life choices, experiences, the things I like and dislike about myself, most of my complexes, what other people think about me, my view of the universe, and 30 percent of all conversations I've had after either four cups of coffee after 2:00 a.m. on a weekday or eight to ten beers on a Thursday or Friday between 11:00 p.m. and midnight.

I flashed back to a college coffeehouse reading. My roommate at the time had invited me, saying if I wanted to write I should put myself out there. At twenty-nine, my presence there was barely legal, and arriving with a stiff gin and tonic in a ginger ale bottle didn't help my tenuous claim to innocence. This was my second visit, and the one where I actually read something.

I don't remember most of the readings. The MC was a contrived personality programmed by a stoned computer-science major and stuffed into a freshman as a fraternity prank. I trusted him more when he was acting, which means he probably has a bright future. The only reader who stuck out was a seventeen-year-old kid brushing against goth and punk subcultures. He was out of place in a room mostly full of actors who couldn't shut up about themselves and soft-spoken writers who were princes and princesses of their internal worlds.[*] He was self-effacing but aggressive, laden with a too-well-thought-out personal philosophy, and just an all-around smart and awkward mess of hormones. His piece was not genius, but his work was searching, assertive, and more than the purely masturbatory work that filled the rest of the night.[†] He put himself out in front of a crowd of people who didn't respect him and he knew it, but he did it and he did it as well as any self-conscious teenager could expect.

I related to him. At seventeen, I was right about there.

I read an old essay called "Men are Stupid, Women are Crazy,"[‡] which always makes young people like me. I owned

---

[*] This is true of me too, except I am the One True God of my internal world, and I am an angry god.

[†] One girl read her diaries from when she was eight. It was entertaining for exactly one tenth of the time she was reading, and you could hear the collective teeth grinding as she gushed over her long-gone cleverness.

[‡] I wrote it long before the book of the same name came out. I stand awkwardly by it as an analysis of social interpretations of what crazy and stupid mean in common parlance, but it's not developed or thoughtful enough to put into print. Or that's what I think, at any rate. I certainly wasn't thinking about the belittling effect it had on women. I'd personally prefer being called crazy over stupid, but in the anti-intellectual hell that is America, I didn't think about how people might pride themselves on that,

the room. They laughed and clapped when I wanted them to, and mobbed me afterward, asking where they could read my work, telling me I understood so much about people. I stood up as straight as I could with my back problems and humbly accepted their accolades, wondering which of the girls I would sleep if she were two years older. I did not linger, for I had a mission. I made a beeline for my seventeen-year-old hero to whom nobody was talking, dragging my new followers with me. I said, "Dude, I liked your piece. Keep writing."

My fan club looked aghast. I took a slug off my gin and tonic, thanked them, and left with my roommate.

When I told this story to my heterosexual lifemate, Jake, he said, "Wow. Why didn't you just wear a cape?" He was completely right. Sure, I wanted to give someone the kind of push people gave me when I was figuring myself out, but I also wanted to selflessly—and publicly—grant him all the benefits of the admiration directed at me, so I could feel, as Jake pointed out, like Superman.

It gets worse. My bout in the nuthouse made it vivid fact that somewhere in the wiring of my brain lies a palpable Jesus complex. I do want to save you all. A part of me wants to suf-

---

and the whole "men are stupid, women are crazy" refrain is solely at the expense of women, since people just adore stupid in this country. There was a whole goddamn ad campaign with slogans like "Smart has plans. Stupid has stories," and "Smart listens to the head. Stupid listens to the heart." This was in 2010. I thought it was a joke.

fer for you, channel your pain, and grant you freedom and eternal life. And another, more evident part of me wants you all to worship me for the next two thousand years as a living god. I like to think of this as boilerplate copy that everyone muses about in their daydreams, the only difference being I put my neurosis on display.

Gil claims my breadth of spirit for my fellow humans is a form of largess rarely seen outside the privileged classes, and probably a form of condescension. My reaction to that is first that that kind of comment is a semicritical kind of thing to say so the speaker can bring me down in their minds and feel better about not being like me, and second that she's probably right, so the paradox is should or do I feel better than everybody else because I think nobody is better than anybody else, and everyone should get a chance?

At my local bar, I'm everybody's last friend. When they've pissed off every other person, made everyone else uncomfortable, made the bar a noticeably worse place and are days away from being kicked out, I'm the only person who still talks to them and says, "Hey, he's just got issues, he's alright sometimes." This particular behavior, as I like to see it, is an undiscriminating acceptance of the human condition. It's also recklessly enabling. I don't believe there are bad people, and barring psychopathy, most of the people considered bad just got poor training for this supposedly ethical and polite society. There are uncountable reasons we grate on one another, and I attempt to ignore them all. It's impossible: I hate with the best of them. Prick me, do I not bleed? Cut me off on the stairway, do I not want to break your stupid fucking face? I estimate that I want to beat up at least one person a day, but I also know it wouldn't help anyone. My acceptance is also un- helpful: If a person is making my bar a worse place for every- one else, they should be told to leave. I just can't be the enforcer.

So why am I like this?

For one, I have an overdeveloped sense of empathy. If I'm around people who are miserable, I'm miserable until I can cheer them up, and I can't do anything but try. This leads me to avoid people who are pathologically miserable, because if I stay around them, I'll just continue to be miserable and try to fix their problem until somebody tells me this girl is bad for me. I resent having this trait, as much as I wish everybody else had it, and since it drags me into a legion of catastrophic emotional situations, I've developed one of the best mental defenses on the planet: total acceptance of everything, all the time.* This is skipping to the end of that "five stages of deal- ing with it" crap, so you're done before it starts.

This relates to the conversation I had with my girlfriend the other day when we were having a beer and she asked me what I'd done to all these women to make them hate me so much, and when was it going to happen to her. Total ac- ceptance includes acceptance of the internal as well as the ex-

---

* Except reggaeton. Seriously? Is there only one one-trick drummer for this entire fucking genre?

ternal, so I'm open with my past and my present, and people tend to see that as extreme emotional vulnerability. It's actually extreme emotional openness, and a means of protecting myself, since if everything's on the table, nothing's under it rattling chains and snapping at toes. This is great for making friends but not so good for romance, since in romance I will state explicitly that I'm not in it for the long haul, but my naked soul lets people feel safer making themselves more vulnerable, and they can't bounce back from problems the way I can, because they were holding on to those rare vintage secrets for a special occasion, whereas I splatter mine all over the internet for fun. So, in the words of Busta Rhymes, I bounce. Others crumble. It's taken a long time to mature enough to keep this from happening, and to learn that you have to be careful with others' emotions, even—or especially—when you think you're being honest.

I was justly punished for most of the terrible things I've done in my life. I was a hideous child, but the lectures and disappointment added up to a passable sense of pleasant versus asshole, and I adapted. Slept with best friend's girlfriend, best friend knocks on my window at 2:00 a.m. and makes me relate the story while he puts cigarettes out on his arm. Slept with my next best friend's ex-girlfriend, he doesn't speak to me for six months while we're living together. There are less sexy things that I won't relate, but the point is psychological torture is an effective teacher, even (or especially) when it can never be condoned as a policy of a just society. The irony is that I'm completely unequipped to execute the kind of punishment that made me a relatively nice person. Not only because of the punishments, but because I've done so many awful things yet maintained the public and private image of a decent human being; therefore a person has to exceed my list of personal betrayals (or kill a bunch of children) before I can question their life choices.

After empathy and punishment, having a lot of terrible things happen to you makes you not want terrible things to happen. After enough psychosis, suicide, death, and failure, you just want the world to be well greased. For instance, after six years of receiving shitty tips as a waiter, I would never tip badly.* If you don't believe in a solution, you believe in keeping things quiet. Never raise the temperature and never start the fight. The horror is real and inevitable, and the best you can do is not contribute to it.

---

* Between writing this and editing it, I did, for the first time in my life, tip badly. Thirty minutes to come over and ask if we were going to order. Thirty minutes to food. Ten minutes to notice we were done. The bill was wrong, charging us for things we didn't order or get. And it wasn't just that visit: every waiter in this place is incompetent and on a cell phone half the time, and all of them being French is no excuse. Service in France is much better. I sent the waiter back to correct the bill and we left our money on the table before he got back. After the bill was corrected, he probably got 10 percent. Yeah, what? What? Choke on it, you French bastard.

I went to a bunch of Quaker schools when I was a kid. If I still play a supporting role in any of my childhood friends' memories, I probably stand out as the kid who invented and ran Beatdown Wednesdays, wherein I selected someone at random and rallied my classmates into chasing them around and beating them up. At a Quaker school. It took a lot of authority figures telling me I was a jerk to curb this behavior, but what I remember is the little plaque in the principal's office that said "Do unto to other as you would have them do unto you." Thankfully, that stuck in my head more than the fascist habits I was teaching myself at the tender age of seven. Later in life, I noticed that people do unto to others as they assume people will do unto them. The people most paranoid about getting robbed are the people most likely to rob you, the people who assume everyone hates them are the most hateful, the people most worried about your stability are the most unstable people. The people most worried about getting hurt are the people most likely to hurt you. They know what they're going to do, and are afraid of people doing it to them.

Above and beyond all the defensive strategies, treating everyone you meet as a complete, probably flawed, and forgivable human being is an offensive strategy, since people tend to act in accordance with the expectations of the people around them. Not the explicit expectations; the actual expectations. Some retail chain once decided to deny its employees pockets in their uniforms. The result was employee theft doubled, because while they said they expect employees not to steal, they assumed they would, and their workforce responded to the assumption. Nothing makes me want a cigarette more than a nonsmoking sign, and being told I'm not allowed off school grounds makes me want to smoke pot in the woods. As a breed, we will wiggle and squirm around every rule, because we know the rule expresses the distrust and condescension of the people imposing it. To paraphrase Paul Tillich, every command erodes the connection between the commander and the commanded, since it encodes a relationship and mocks the trust that makes a relationship work. To demand that people act a certain way lest they be judged is to ask for a problem. I have such a problem with it I've quit jobs and left states at the hint of it.

We all look at our own thoughts and assume, no matter how much we claim otherwise, that other people's thoughts follow the same patterns. As much as I try to find and figure other people's patterns, I know I'm only peeking at them from the closet of my own mind. We casually imbue the most complex and variable organ in the world with a structure similar to our own three-pound lump of gray matter, even when we know they cannot possibly be the same. In doing this, we assume that when others err, they had a thought process like ours but made the wrong decision because of some underlying weakness, and we pass judgment. The more likely scenario is that they were equipped with a different system of values and developed a different hierarchy of need and desire. That hierarchy changes moment to moment, and sometimes a desire gets poorly weighed against the future. That's certainly my defense, so, at least in part, I don't judge because not judging is a coping mechanism. Insisting there can be no judgment means I cannot be judged.

I don't condone or condemn via any existential basis, and I refuse to be condemned or condoned. We fear in others what we see in ourselves, and if I fear nothing in others, I get to sleep at night, no matter what I've done, no matter what I'm going to do. There may be good things and bad things in my future, but I put nobody beneath me, and I won't let anybody put me beneath them. I won't make you my bitch, because that presumes the possibility of me being somebody's bitch.

And I am nobody's bitch.

DATING 101: MEDIAN

JG was devastatingly intelligent. She had a katana-like mind: Sometimes I'd go for a touché before realizing my hand was missing. She had no cares for the assumptions and expectations of the world that couldn't be backed by data. She had a smile that could make a psychopath run home to masturbate with his tears.

She was a little culturally myopic. Later in our friendship I made a comparison to Jimi Hendrix and she said, "Who's that?"

"What? Who's who?"

"Who's Jimi Hendrix? Is he recent?"

"Are you joking? You don't know who Jimi Hendrix is? Really?"

"Never heard of him."

"Oh my God we're fixing this right now."

She laughed at me as I dug for a pen and paper to write it down. "People always get the most upset when you don't know about their favorite bands."

"This isn't about my favorite music, it's freaking Jimi Hendrix. He invented hard rock, for God's sake. He changed guitar."

I mean come on, Jimi Hendrix? There are villages in India that don't know the British were ever there, and I bet there's a kid in one of them who will tell you "Machine Gun" was a tighter critique of U.S. war policy than the Woodstock rendition of "The Star-Spangled Banner." It's like not knowing about Beethoven.

Point is, my first date with her was kind of like a date with a really charming anthropologist from Neptune. I found myself having to explain things that I never thought I'd have to explain or defend, like why high school sucked, why people tend to assume homeschooled kids are religious nuts, why I like cats, why I drink too much, etc. It was disarming and fun, and I probably learned more about myself that night than I did about her.

I wasn't sure about my chances, but I suspected they were slim because she was a nonsmoker. I've dated many nonsmokers, but if my soul mate was presented to me during a meteor shower with the "Hallelujah Chorus" spontaneously bursting from the hills while the voice of God said, "Peter, this is the one, trust me, I'm fucking God," and she said smoking was a deal breaker, I'd understand.*

---

* I mean, I'd try to quit, but that never goes well for me.

I went for the kiss anyway. I'd give it a six, but it had just enough passion that I figured we were on our way.

Two days later, we're making plans for another date via AIM, and she comes up with this: "Want to go to a party with a bunch of my friends?"

Not being particularly suave or comfortable back then, I did not take this as, "Wow, she already wants me to meet her friends," but more, "I'm going to have to talk to a room full of strangers for three hours?" So I said, "That sounds really uncomfortable." She came back with, "Oh. That surprises me. Well, we can do something else."

She followed up a second later with, "Not a date thing, though."

It takes a particular skill to fail something that wasn't a test. She may have not wanted to date me at all, but there was no indication of it before I demonstrated my lack of gumption. She wasn't the testing type. She just wanted to do this and wanted to bring me, and analyzed my response for precisely what it was: I wanted to be alone with her to charm her on easy terms, and didn't have the balls to compete for her attention, and wasn't relaxed or smart enough to understand it wasn't a competition. I think she was on the fence about me in her mind: Cute *enough*, smart *enough*, maybe charming *enough*, let's wait and see if he's at least a little outside the norm.

Not this guy.

For some reason, teachers liked me in high school. Except for one, apparently, which I only know because a family friend, who was also a teacher at my high school, told me, but they wouldn't tell me which one. In retrospect, I think I know who it was, but at the time, I had to sit around worrying about whom and why. She shouldn't have told me anything, but I'm sure it's one of those automatic twitches pseudogrownups have that make them try to reinforce the concept of amorphous, anonymous disapproval in children. Then again, another friend of mine told me one of the girls in my class at Mount Holyoke was a man-hater, and thus, predictably, hated me, but my friend wouldn't say who it was, which is fair, but she shouldn't have said anything in the first place. Her motivation was less clear, but to the both of you, if you're reading this, you know who you are, and in the future, keep it to yourselves.

I digress. Most of my teachers seemed to like me, and two of them liked me enough to get me into the class trip to Italy after I had dropped out of high school. Bear in mind that as my mother was driving me out of the parking lot on the last day of my sophomore year and of high school in general, I rolled down the window, leaned out, and screamed, "Rot in Hell, motherfuckers!" at the collected studentry and any teachers who were leaving early.

Six months later, I'm sixteen and in Italy, with a bunch of high school students. It's an interesting mix; there are two girls I would have sacrificed a toe to sleep with, a few people I know, and a few I don't. The room arrangement that includes me is out of a cheap bromance comedy: I, the dropout semi-goth, angsty poet wannabe, am tossed in with the six-foot-two superjock and the son of a liberal radio host whose teen-age rebellion consisted of becoming a young Republican who wore a tie to school every day and looked like he would turn forty at a moment's notice. It was exactly like a sitcom, and that was just our room; the rest of the group did not disappoint, being mostly theater kids.

I don't remember a single name of anybody on this trip. Actually, one: Gail, one of the teachers. Other than that, I don't recall any of the students' names, not the other teacher (I want to say Beth, but it's a shot in the dark), not the Italian tour guide, not any of the surprising number of people we met in our travels. I don't remember much of what we saw, aside from the gondolier in Venice falling off his boat, some pigeons, and a dome or two in Florence. Or maybe they were in Rome. Also, beer in the vending machines.

The first lesson was that despite my exit from high school and the natural smugness that accompanies being a well-read dropout, I was still woefully unequipped to play the social game. To nutshell the coming stories, the girl I respected and wanted to date was in love with my jock roommate, who was in love with the New Yoik Doll, whom everybody wanted to fuck and who wouldn't give anybody the time of day because why should she, and I hadn't the faintest idea what to do with the theater kids' overemotive and underage-drunk interactions, except sip brandy and smoke cigarillos on poker nights. As was to become a theme for many years, I ended up dragging one of them home and putting him to bed after he'd done a full American tourist at an otherwise quiet bar in Florence. He spent the walk lamenting some girl not loving him enough. I dropped him off at his room, he thanked me, drunkenly and profusely, and I told him, verbatim: "You don't know jack shit about love." I'm equal parts embarrassed and proud of this moment as the pseudoadult I am today. On the one hand, I was right, since nobody under twenty knows much about anything. On the other hand, that was the only time anybody could be as stupidly and completely in love as he was and I had been. On the Beeblebrox hand, I spoke out of a ripening angst over my first childhood love and my first childhood girlfriend, who were not the same people, so despite being almost a year away from my first sexual encounter, I felt I knew the paths of the heart. Or at least the sand traps, if not the fairway, much less the green. You know where this metaphor is going.

Whatever I thought I knew, I was wrong, but not necessarily more wrong than he was, and I was less drunk, so I call it a win.

Since our roommate was an insane young Republican, who either lied about not masturbating, or—in the far more terrifying scenario—didn't, the jock and I became fast friends. A year after this trip, back in standard Bar Harbor, Maine, America, he would mock me in front of his jock friends at his graduation. By then I'd stopped caring about what the high school popularati thought of me, but it still hurt. I know why he did it, and I hope he grew out of it, because I liked him. If he didn't, I feel sorry for him, because people like me think of pity as one of the finest forms of revenge. Dick.

Anyway. We bonded for some unholy reason, and stuck fairly close while the infatuation triangle developed between him, Cancer Girl, and New Yoik Doll.

I don't remember which came first. I believe Cancer Girl, because she was in the same group as Coast Guard Girl, which people close to me might interpret as a euphemism disguising disdain, except the other options are Alien Neck Girl, which just sounds weird, and Girl I Wanted to Have Sex With a Decade After Meeting Her is a little wordy (and my girlfriend would disapprove, I'm sure). I've lost the picture I took as proof, but for some reason she could suck in the skin on her neck around her tendons to a point where you wondered if she wasn't born of this world. She also loved her country, which is mine too, but I hold no great fondness for it, while she would happily place her life on the line to protect it. Despite this, she and I had the best rapport out of any of my relationships on this trip, but she was from a faraway land (New Hampshire) and since I can't remember her name, even the modern age of unparalleled stalking abilities leaves me with so few leads I don't even try.

Cancer Girl had survived cancer, and gave me my first personal introduction to a person who put the moves on life because she had come so close to losing it. She seemed a touch on the crazy side, but not excessively crazy for a teenager. I fell for her too, but she was infatuated with Jock, and taking life by the testicles failed her in this effort, because he just thought she wasn't as hot as New Yoik Doll.

New Yoik Doll was exactly the kind of girl men like me often go to jail over. Stunningly hot, obviously young, developed enough to frame in a viewfinder and post on Facebook with the caption, "Maybe jail's worth it, amirite?" to attract a slew of not-self-conscious-enough comments to the tune of "LMFAO!!!111eleven of course, man, of course!" I wouldn't say she knew her precise effect on the men around her, but she knew that she could ramble on about whatever pointless nonsense was in her head at any moment and every guy around her would smile and nod and laugh and agree with her. Given that we were all teenagers, and Jock and I were from Maine while she was from New Yoik, she probably could have gotten us goose-stepping for a few blocks before we questioned ourselves.

This girl and her group of New Yoik friends only started hanging out with us because I approached them, and I only did that when I realized they were speaking English, as their Brooklyn accents were so thick it just sounded like a bunch of swallowed consonants and dragging vowels and I thought they were French. Once they were on the bus and I had sussed out a few English words, I figured what the hell, as, even for me, being in another country mutes some of the self-consciousness involved in being an awkward teenager, so I regaled them with the definition of *wicked* and how people are weird, and we merged groups. Ultimately, my frustration with their frivolousness and my inability to even attempt to have sex with them soured the relationship, and they gave me my second most unfortunate nickname after "Petey," namely, "Rat Boy." It's as accurate a nickname as I've ever had, since even now a few days without a shave, a bad haircut, and a light rain leave me looking like a rat. Still, it cut. Soon after making cross-state introductions, I found I preferred to spend my time with Cancer and Coast Guard, who were more interested in the New England frivolousness I was used to.

Cancer pursued Jock with a vengeance. He did what most guys do when a woman gives them uninvited attention: assume she's nuts and run after a younger, unattainable girl from Brooklyn. But that would come later. Before that, we discovered our teachers thought it would be great idea to let us loose in a bunch of dance clubs. Apparently every other teacher of every other school also thought it would be a good idea, so Jock and I were invited to hang out with the girls in the New Hampshire group at some local spot where all the cool people several years older than us hung out. Nobody else came, since the theater kids were busy trying to inbreed and Young Republican wouldn't know what to do. So the two of us got the entire tour bus to ourselves as a ride to the club.

We sprawled out in the back and discussed how many other middle-class teenagers from Maine were getting personal transport to a club in Italy that night, or ever would. We decided none, and clinked our champagne glasses. There may not have been champagne, but there are only three witnesses and the driver didn't speak English, so even if this is a padded recollection, I'm going with it.

Sketchy is just shy of a perfect description for the club we entered after leaving our perfect transport. I paid twelve dollars for a Coke, which in my experience up till then suggested there would be a waiter coming shortly who didn't need to write down my order to remember it. There were corners full of broken glass, there was probably a lot of cocaine, and I saw a woman being manhandled by a pop-collared twenty-year-old only to be saved from the situation by an equally pop-collared twenty-year-old who proceeded to hang all over her, while she wore an expression suggesting that she would deal with being groped as long as she wasn't being beaten. I saw three fights almost start between various collars, and then they started accosting our women.

I say "our women" specifically because this was a pretty raw and foreign assault on people we cared about, and it was giving a face and a situation to our unmanaged and, in the traditional American style, unexamined and unadmitted man-feelings. The Italian kids had no such problems. We attempted to intervene, but the girls, being surrounded by incredibly hot Italian guys, just waved us off and said everything was fine. We tried going to our chaperones, but no, no, it's fine, despite the fact that a couple of the Italian kids tried to set fire to our hair while we were dancing. So we sat in a corner and watched, knowing the situation was about to get out of control, unable to get anyone to believe us, itching to throw down, and savagely outnumbered. We were the only guys in our group, and we were just then understanding and dreading how awful we could potentially be, and we were watching others of our gender become exactly that awful.

The outcome was a bit of a blur, but basically, one of the girls was grinding between three or four of the Italian guys, and—probably because she was a fifteen-year-old girl—she decided that maybe a few of those hands were in inappropriate places, and tried to get away from them. They weren't so eager to let her go. Fortunately she got the attention of her friends, and they managed to free her and everybody rushed out. The chaperone later said, "It got a little out of hand in there, nobody saw it coming, we're all okay." Jock and I just looked at each other and went home. I tore off my button-down shirt in frustration and to express some kind of aggression. Jock was already in bed, but said he wanted to do the same thing, but he only had one good shirt. The homoeroticism of the situation was lost on us both.

Try as we might, we never convinced the girls that, at least in that brief, tarnished moment, we were right, and they should have listened to us. We eventually gave up.

Before we parted ways with the New Hampsters, I passed notes from Cancer to Jock while trying to subtly suggest she look elsewhere. In the end, she gave me one of those hematite rings to give to him. I didn't want to bug him about it at the time, so I just wore it after our groups parted ways, leaving him unmolested in his pursuit of New Yoik Doll.

One of the moments that sticks in my brain in that painful tale is a late-night conversation, probably one of my first 3:00 a.m., insane-with-caffeine-and-exhaustion conversations. We were listening to her, or at least I was listening to her, saying those little agreeing things guys say when they don't give a damn but are pretending they do so they can keep staring at a girl. I could tell Jock was trying to use his body language to actively suggest sex, but to no avail. She was using her body language to suggest she was hot and we should hang on every banal, barely comprehensible topic of the current ten seconds. Despite Jock's impressive stature and better looks, he was as powerless as I in front of this future model from a savvier city. He may have had a better chance if I hadn't been around, but I wasn't going to give up my shot. We were temporary, cross-caste bros by that point (about ten minutes past the second half of act two), but "bros before hoes" is utter bullshit, unless the hoes in question are literally prostitutes and you can buy more. If you pay attention to classical literature, you'll notice men only kill one another over other men when the other men are dead, while they merrily kill one another over women who are still alive, and sometimes over women who just got lost on the way somewhere. Think about it.

After that conversation, I essentially cut ties with the New Yoikers by responding to the head girl's question, "Why don't you do what I say?" with, "Because I don't like you." I got to know the theater kids, and thought about New Hampshire. At some inebriated point, we tried to think of all the words that ended in "-ation." I'll give you a hint: there are a lot of them, and, ironically in this particular venture, only one of them is masturbation.

The other club we went to was supposedly *the* dance club of Europe, so we figured we'd give it a shot, even after the previous club. We all got in on this one, and danced the night away. This is the scene of one of my proudest moments, wherein I convinced the girls from another tour group that I was Italian. If you're sixteen and on a trip to Italy, here's what you do:

1. Find a confused huddle of girls speaking English.

2. Walk up to them.

3. Say, "*Baila? Baila?*"

4. Wait for them to say, "Sorry, we don't speak Italian."

5. Say, "Oh, Americanos! I speak, ey huh, American. Come, we dance, *baila* is dance."

6. Grab one and dance with her.

7. Do not run into her at the airport two weeks later when both your tours are going home.

Eventually the one I grabbed decided she'd had enough grinding with this subpar fake Italian, and I danced to "Smells Like Teen Spirit" by myself. At some point I was clapping to a shitty techno song and my standard pewter ring hit the hematite ring and shattered it. I realized I was an asshole. Then I got a drink and realized I was okay with that.

This was the moment when the seed of modern Pete was planted, though its shoots would wilt for years to come.

On the way home in the airport, I think the girls from the club actually liked me more when they discovered I was a lying American. In my first moment of cool, I shrugged when they found me out and said, "Hey, who wouldn't?" and was rewarded with giggles.

After this, I owed my teacher a hundred bucks, and fifty to one of the theater kids, which I fully intend to pay if I ever see him again. As I mentioned, Jock wouldn't admit to knowing me when he got back with his jock friends. I never reconnected with Cancer or Coast Guard, and never intended to see the New Yoikers again. In fact, the only person I had any serious contact with afterward was Young Republican, and it was an unfulfilling relationship.

The plane ride back was long. The bus ride was probably longer, and on this bus ride I sat next to another girl whose name I can't remember, and whom I would never see again. I think I'd spoken to her a few times on the trip. She was tall, at least five ten, with long blond hair. She was shy, and quiet. I hadn't noticed before, but she was pretty behind a wool coat-sweater and glasses that were too big for her face. She smiled easily. We talked about music and movies, and I realized I was getting sick, and my ears hadn't unclogged yet from our flight's descent. It was late, and we were tired. I asked if I could put my head on her shoulder, and she said yes. We rested against the window and watched the rain until we fell asleep.

24 HOURS OF PRIVILEGE

This is the approximated average of what goes through my brain every day.

9:00 a.m.

My iPhone alarm goes off. I hit snooze, secure in the knowledge that any catastrophe severe enough to affect my work in a way I couldn't deal from a random computer would be severe enough that I'd have to stay home anyway.

9:09 a.m.

My iPhone alarm goes off. I hit snooze, secure in the knowledge that I do white-collar work for a tech startup, so I can get there, you know, morningish, as long as I'm sober.

9:18 a.m.

My iPhone alarm goes off. I hit snooze, because . . . I dunno. So comfy.

9:53 a.m.

Dammit. Slept through the snooze for half an hour. I really was going to be on time today. I glance out the window to see if the weather could excuse working from home. Sunny. Damn. May as well get to it.

9:55 a.m.

Because nobody cares what I look like, I unselfconsciously pull on the jeans and T-shirt I threw on the floor eight hours ago. If anyone notices, they'll chalk it up to my manly laziness. One minute later, I finish my morning routine by chugging a liter of free tap water, waving a toothbrush at my face, and glancing in the mirror to make sure my hair isn't sticking up. Hair looks good. I congratulate myself on being tall.

9:57 a.m.

I glide past my mailbox, which is probably full. I check it about once a week, pull out the mail, flip through it, and stuff it back in, unless it's too full, in which case I just carry a handful straight to the trash cans outside my building. I know that no piece of mail without a handwritten address will affect my life in any meaningful way. I don't rely on physical correspondence with any private or government agency to get my food and utilities, and my creditors can suck it. If it's important, someone will call me.

10:05 a.m.

Halfway to the train. Only have to dodge a couple of slow people today. Why the hell can't everybody move as quickly and gracefully as tall, healthy thirty-year-olds in comfortable shoes?

10:07 a.m.

A loud conversation signals danger to me. I hate loud people. Just trying to draw attention to themselves. Why can't they just accept the natural respect granted them by other human beings? Doesn't everybody get that? I glance in the direction of the noise and see the conversationalists are black. Damn. I don't hate black people, I hate loud people. But black people in America tend to be louder. No, dammit, certain cultures tend to be louder. I dislike loud white people, too. Like Italians. Is that racist? They're white, so it's cool, right? What's with loud people? Is it a cultural thing? Economic? Why can't everybody just shut up so I don't have to think about this? Jesus, I don't care what you need to do to get by in your neighborhood, just keep it out of my brain space.

10:09 a.m.

Rounding the White Castle. Still hung up on whether or not I'm racist. I have black friends. Bah, classic excuse for a racist. I repeat the word *nigger* in my head several times to be sure it still makes me uncomfortable. It does. Good. Not racist. I stop thinking about it.

10:12 a.m.

I swap my shades for my glasses in the subway for easier reading on my Kindle, which I just loaded up with another batch of random books. People don't read enough. Why doesn't everybody have a kindle with three thousand dollars of literature on it? As I put on my glasses, it occurs to me that people still associate glasses with intelligence. My genetic shortcomings are advantageous to my career.

10:20 a.m.

On the train, looking over 90 percent of everybody's heads. I'm still feeling bad about going off on a long-rehearsed rant about a former employer being a "short, awkward sociopath" to a friend who was slightly shorter than the aforementioned employer. I learned at OkCupid that height is for men what weight is for women, and I knew that some men were uncomfortable with being short, and my former employer had a very tall friend, so in my occasional rage fantasy, I spout this to his face as a remark to leverage possible self-image issues. My friend, without blinking, says, "He's not that short," and I feel like an ass. It takes me back to another friend who was standing on a chair for a show and said, "So this is what it's like to be tall," and I looked at him and realized I didn't even know he was short. I don't notice anyone's height unless they're at least four inches taller than me. I just see "people my height," "giant freaks," and "everybody else." It didn't occur to me people might be concerned about their height until I was in my late twenties.

10:40 a.m.

At Starbucks, reading various things off signs and menus and newspapers while I stand in line. As long as something is mostly in English, I can read it. I grew up with people reading and explaining complex literature, in houses that had multiple rooms dedicated to storing books. There are few topics of nonfiction or styles of prose my upper-middle-class childhood didn't expose me to, and that left me with an enormous vocabulary and a broad system of background knowledge with which to tackle almost anything. Jeez, doesn't everybody have that? Childhood is for reading, right? I shake my head, then use my overeducated middle-class vocabulary to read the back of a CD entitled *Music for Little Hipsters.*

10:42 a.m.

I smoke a cigarette outside my office. Smoking is the only thing I do anymore that makes me feel awkward around strangers, and my office is on a particularly bad street for that, with a trickle of people wandering by with kids and dogs and a never-ending series of trucks making deliveries. I hide my cigarettes from children, try not to blow smoke in people's faces, and stand in an area calculated to annoy the smallest number of people. I know it's hopeless, since my bouts with quitting taught me that a normal nose can smell a cigarette from half a block away, but I try to be a good little smoker, because I know I'm killing myself and I should quit and I don't want to bother anyone. At the same time, I'm waiting for some asshole to say, "You know cigarettes are bad for you?" or, "That's disgusting," so I can tell them to fuck off, because I know at least a few people are thinking it, and at least one person shoots me a dirty look every day. I spend most of my cigarette breaks in this state of being apologetic and angry at the same time. Must suck to feel that way about something you have no control over, amirite?

10:46 a.m.

Made it to the office. Checking e-mail. No emergencies. Next, in order, I check The Doghouse Diaries, xkcd, smbc, what-if.xkcd, Facebook, Twitter, and reddit. Gotta ease into a desk job, you know?

11:00 a.m.

Time for the 11:00 a.m. shit. I hear regularity is a sign of good health, which boggles my mind, considering my lifestyle, and especially my past lifestyle. I guess it helped to be born into a family with no genetic or historical markers indicating susceptibility to any known disease. I play my turn in Scrabble on my phone and wash up.

11:10 a.m. to 1:50 p.m.

Work. It's generally not that hard, despite it being a job that evolved out of a hobby. I developed lots of hobbies while frittering away the seven years of on-and-off college my parents paid for me to occasionally attend, so odds were one of them would turn into money. I was finding myself, you know?

2:00 p.m.

Lunch! I toy with the idea of picking up a sandwich and eating it on my desk, but decide to do my usual routine of sitting down at a restaurant and reading for an hour over a gourmet meal and a glass of wine, because I can. I bring up Yelp and peruse restaurants. I've been searching for the perfect meatball for the last few years, because I found it once in a Holiday Inn on 31st Street. Unfortunately, the restaurant closed, and nothing else has passed muster since. I suspect they were veal, which troubles me morally. I have time to think about the morality of my eating habits, so might as well. Unless I accidentally find the perfect meatball and start suspecting it's veal and adopt a Google No Evil policy. I look longingly at a few veal recipes, but can't bring myself to consume a tortured animal with foreknowledge. I feel good about myself. I decide on an Irish beef stew, pack up my Kindle, and head out.

3:00 p.m. to 8:00 p.m.

Work, chitchat, a dash of Facebook. A great deal of chatter in the IRC chat room, equal parts mutual tech support, politics, and mom jokes. We joke about how diverse we are: We have an Asian, an Indian, and a couple of black people, although one of them is Canadian so he doesn't really count. Hell, we even have two girls. In a PROGRAMMING chat room. Look at our goddamn rainbow of hands across Benetton.

8:10 p.m.

On the train home, wondering what I'll look like when I get old. Aging well so far, despite the smoking. If I quit, I could probably attract grad students in my late fifties as long as they had daddy issues. I pause for a moment to consider labeling uncountable relationships as daddy-issue situations, because of course "daughter issues" would be creepy. Seems like a complicated thing to think about after a long day in front of a computer. I stop thinking about it when an unusual number of attractive women get on the train at Union Square, and I have to focus on trying not to eye-rape them, because that would be rude. I congratulate myself on overcoming this struggle. At no point do I concern myself with if and how people are looking at me.

8:30 p.m.

Walking to the bar, enjoying the fantasy of someone attacking me so I can kung fu them into recognizing that I have taught them an important lesson about dignity. Of course this is just a fantasy because I've never been attacked and don't expect to be. I've walked through dark factory parking lots a mile from the nearest streetlight and the worst that's happened is somebody told me I wasn't allowed to take pictures of the facility. I can't recall ever being in a place where I was scared because of the way I look. Once I was seeing a girl who lived in Harlem, and when I got off the subway I looked around and thought, *Wow, I'm the only white person I can see. So this is how black people feel in Maine. Neat!*

9:00 p.m.

I'm on my second glass of wine at the bar. It's on the tab that I run once a month, that I'm allowed to have because whenever somebody mentions it's hitting mid–triple digits, I can pull out a card and pay it, due to the hobby-job I complain about that pays me more money than most of the people I know because the market is demanding people who can make birds fly into pipes. Nobody has considered me a threat to their business since I cut my hair.

10:00 p.m.

I arrive home with my backup bottle of wine, since I need to get home before the Chinese delivery place closes. I know no one will judge me for the wine besides my parents, because I'm doing stuff for the economy or something. I have a 10 to 8 job: I'm contributing. Doing my part. Where's the corkscrew?

10:30 p.m.

I'm trying to decide what to turn on: Xbox, PlayStation 3, PlayStation 4, Apple TV, Nintendo, or OUYA. I've actually run out of toys to buy. I congratulate myself on my restraint.

I feel like I should use my Xbox more, since I bought it to deal with the emotional trauma of a bunch of people getting fired at my old job. Not me, of course. Can't buy an Xbox when you've just lost your job. I bought some indie games to support indie developers, because that justifies everything. I download *Oblivion,* and commence the noble pursuit of playing a game on the gigantic TV I bought to prove I was an adult.

11:46 p.m.

Getting kind of late. I brush my teeth and congratulate myself on getting to the hygiene part of the evening before the evening turned into wee hours. I laugh at the phrase "wee hours" because I went to some liberal arts schools and we always laughed about the wee hours when we were crushing our pills and smoking our joints. The word *lamentable* echoes in my head, and I feel proud of knowing what it means, because I went to high school with people who didn't.

12:30 a.m.

I smoke a cigarette and look at the letter tacked to my wall from Jose Armando Vasquez Lopez. He's a child I briefly sponsored through Children International. My debit card expired during this sponsorship. I tell myself I didn't know it expired, but I'm lying. I had the right intentions, didn't I? Somebody else sponsored him after me before I got the chance to write back. Not my fault, I was giving away money, wasn't I? I feel like a bastard every time I see it, but I don't take it off the wall. I did something, briefly, and here's my proof. Also, it reminds me to guilt myself. I congratulate myself on being a good person.

1:12 a.m.

Definitely working from home tomorrow. Need to put the finishing touches on an essay displaying the self-awareness that totally excuses me from being complacent in the system of extortion and slavery that produces most of my toys. As long as you know your ironic T-shirts are produced by child labor, that's cool, right? It's just a more worldly irony.

1:34 a.m.

I consider going off the grid for a week. Because the grid is the problem, and I can leave it for a few days and find myself again. Because there will always be a job waiting for a tall straight white boy who knows python is both a snake and a language. I can take time away from it all, because I don't need to scramble at the hint of protein. I don't need to worry about next week because there will be a safety net for me, no matter what I do, no matter where I am. I'm the all-American boy anyone would weep for if I ended up on the back of a milk carton.

2:04 a.m.

I feed my cats and give them catnip. They reward me with purrs. I consider shaving, but I'm a bit drunk, and it won't affect my job, and I'm just attractive enough to not have to think about how attractive I am. I put *Buffy* on Netflix and fall asleep to an episode of season five.

9:00 a.m.

My iPhone alarm goes off. I hit snooze, because I don't have to give a shit. I congratulate myself on not caring.

FOR FUCK'S SAKE, IRENE

I hear about the storm for the first time on August 23rd. It is a bad day. I spill water on my laptop before I've finished my morning coffee. Having done this before, I yank the cables out, turn it off, soak up what I can with a paper towel, and leave it to dry. A coworker suggests I get a big bag of rice and stick my laptop in it. Sounds good to me, but I think in the future this will be an insult.

I have an office laptop. Had I spilled water on that, I would have handed it to my boss, shrugged, and had a replacement by the end of the week. I prefer my own computer because it's faster, smaller, and already tweaked out with the hundreds of settings and programs and shortcuts I install on all my computers. Still, at least the office laptop works as a plan B.

Four of us get lunch, apparently in an earthquake-free sushi zone, since none of us felt the Virginia quake that rocked, or at least nudged, the office while we were out. We discuss disaster in our Skype group chat, and I idly check the weather and discover there's a hurricane on its way. I submit this information to the chat room, prefacing the news with "This is our real problem" in the hopes of strengthening social ties. I am promptly rewarded with a "Holy fuck."

I congratulate myself on breaking interesting news to the workplace.

August 24th

When I first try to turn my laptop back on, it seems that the shift key is broken and stuck in the on position, forcing me to plug in a keyboard to type in my password. I discover that even if you can type and use the mouse, a permanently pressed shift key makes a computer unusable. In an attempt to open a utility program, I open fifty-six other programs, including the entire Adobe Suite and all my video editing software.

The next time I try to use the computer, the keyboard and the touch pad are completely dead. I consider what lie to tell as I cart the defunct machine to the nearest Apple Super Special Bespectacled 200+ IQ Middle-Class White Polymath, who I know will tell me he has to send it to Texas. I tell him I have no idea what happened to my computer, I just left it open and it wasn't working when I came back from lunch. He takes it and says they'll call with a diagnosis in a couple of days.

August 25th

My girlfriend and I realize we've somehow promised to attend four different events in two boroughs on the 27th. Since neither of us particularly enjoys doing anything more complicated than drinking wine and pausing *Mad Men* to argue about gender roles, the prediction of catastrophic winds requiring us to stay home comes as a relief. We write cheerful apologies to everyone and start stocking wine.

I run into my roommate after work and tell him to make sure the fans and ACs are out of the windows before he goes to his Saturday night bartending shift.

"Because of electricity?" he asks.

I blink.

"No, because of the hurricane."

"Whaaat?"

"There's a giant fucking hurricane hitting us Saturday night."

"Noooo. Really?"

"Dude, how do you function?"

August 26th

Four bottles of wine so far.

I start taping my windows, but then I pause and think about the physics of a chair hurtling through a window at 70 mph. I go to the IRC chartroom full of computer-genius friends who answer all my programming questions and let me pretend I'm qualified to do my job. They direct me to the NOAA website, which informs me that taping windows is pointless. I am shamed, because I always figured this was the right thing to do based on an *X-Files* episode I saw six years ago.

The weather reports are oscillating between a tropical storm and a category 1 hurricane hitting the New York coast. The most vulnerable parts of the city are being evacuated.

The Apple tech calls to inform me he'll need to send my computer to Texas. I tell him I'll pick it up and take my chances. When I get to the store, the tech asks me if I'm sure I didn't spill anything on it. I display every single clichéd body-language indicator of lying and try to cover it up with a half-laugh and shrug.

"Dude, I have no idea. I went to lunch, came back, and my computer was fried."

He nods, then looks me in the eye.

"Do you have any enemies?"

I laugh for real this time. Enemies? Are there really gainfully employed thirtysomethings with relationships in the enemy category? I guess there must be, because he's completely serious. It seems like a paranoid way to live. I take my computer home and put it on the windowsill.

August 27th

I wake up early, for no particular reason, and try my computer. It works just long enough to tell me the mayor has declared a state of emergency. Like the rest of the hipsters, it takes this to get me to start preparing, on the eve of the hurricane. I expect I will face the apocalypse the same way I deal with Christmas: "What, it's the 23rd already?"

The information superswamp is viscous with opinions. It's an even split between those who say nothing's going to happen and those who say the New York City metropolitan area is finally going to get what it deserves. The summation of all these arguments is preordained, since disasters have one of two meanings after they happen: either everybody's asking why we were so worried or asking why we didn't worry enough. I read a comment online that says: "when it just turns out to be a light rain all those New Yorkers are going to feel stoooooopid lol (yeah I know I spelled 'stoopid' wrong lol)." This suggests that joining the debate will make me dumber, so I ignore it. Since preparing for this storm consists of cleaning things I should have cleaned a month ago, stocking food I'll eat in any event, taking the ACs we don't need anymore out of the windows, and buying a flashlight I should already own, my efforts don't feel especially stoopid.

I wake up my girlfriend and we try to pick up water at the local dollar emporium, the go-to market for cheap plastic junk. They have a sign on the door reading WE HAVE NO WATER, FLASHLIGHTS, OR D BATTERIES. We shrug and look for plastic containers of some kind. We settle on four one-gallon bottles of knockoff orange soda, figuring we can dump them and fill them with water. When we get back and start pouring their contents in the sink, we realize we've erred. The smell is nauseating and, try as we might, we can't wash out the remnant odor. We give up, fill them with water, and decide we'll make my roommate drink them in case of emergency, since he's still asleep and not helping. We fill the fifteen empty wine bottles on the counter with more water and call it good.

Next we empty the fridge, in case of a power outage, which seems the most likely problem we'll have to deal with. I'll spare the details of the ordeal and sum up with this: It needed to be done, there was one item of food in a plastic container that could no longer be identified, and we fully expected tentacles to be squirming out of the outdoor trash can by morning.

Next task was to find a flashlight and pick up more wine. We'd been warned against candles, in case of a broken gas line, so a flashlight was paramount. Since finding a flashlight for sale was unlikely at this juncture, I asked my roommate if he had a hookup. He said he didn't, but recommended looking for glow sticks, in a stroke of genius that could only be achieved by someone who still went clubbing. My girlfriend and I began the quest for glow sticks.

There was a popular story going around that Brooklynites were at no loss for water, but rather clogging the liquor store queues. This appears to be bullshit by the time we hit our third bodega. The lines are wrapping the blocks with people buying batteries and food. There's water in a number of places, although, biblically, no bread. The lines for alcohol seem no worse than an average Saturday afternoon.

In the host of dime and dollar stores we visit, no one shouts. No one fights or shoves or hoards personal space, despite the pervasive and strange emotion equal parts concern, dismissiveness, and excitement. New York moves like lava, slowly and destructively rolling over itself with the look of a river that's never changed course. Every inhabitant waits for the moment that the city has spent its life foreshadowing. The possibility that the moment has arrived draws out each facet of every human in staggered relief. The shoppers joke about the lack of batteries, tsk and sigh and catch themselves and keep control in the press of humanity brought to focus.

Flashlights are nowhere in sight. We eventually find a store selling bike running lights, which take AAA batteries and cost half as much as a real flashlight. We buy two sets, six packs of batteries, and fourteen glow sticks.

Mission accomplished, we head home just as the first rains begin. Eventually, they ease enough for us to notice we're at an intersection home to a scrap-metal yard, a gas station, and a glass factory. We half-expect Michael Bay to be in front of us, licking his lips, a trembling hand reaching for an ignition button.

On a street of railroad apartment buildings, we notice a handful of people smoking at the entrances. They don't speak, or pantomime the motions of boredom. They watch the sky, alone, signaling their existence, and little else.

We pick up four more bottles of wine and more cigarettes, drop them at home, and head for the bar.

The wind is picking up, the rain is coming and going, and everybody's getting drunk as we watch New Jersey wash away on the closed-captioned TVs. Outside, I smoke with some old friends I barely see, and ask if anyone else is a little excited. They're evenly split, but whatever the motivation, everybody's eyes have a little sparkle of wanting to see and/or survive what might come.

My girlfriend and I go home early and survey our preparations. We have fifteen liters plus four gallons of water, eight bottles of wine, six packs of cigarettes, three cans of dry-roasted cashews, a cupboard full of canned peas, pears, peaches, and pineapple, a fridge with the evening's meal of bread, cheese, and mango, and a sword. We're ready for anything. Even irony.

We stay up as late as we can, but it's hotter than usual, and there's no AC. She goes to bed around three. I want to gauge the wind to see if we should sleep in the kitchen, away from the windows. Nothing seems to be happening. At four-thirty in the morning, I give up and join her in bed. The bathroom fan is running when I fall asleep.

August 28th

This was supposed to be it.

This was supposed to be the winds of karma and trees tearing from the ground to crash through our walls and windows. The oceans would rise and punish us for our hubris; the streets would be a river sweeping slightly-more-expensive-than-necessary cars into the sea.

Instead, it's a beautiful day. Supposedly the wind got interesting around five in the morning, and the bar owners couldn't drive home. Everybody else missed it. The parks were a green fall, leaves covering the paths somewhat less alarmingly than when the July heat wave ended and the temperature drop made half of them turn brown and fall off three months ahead of schedule. Every other state in the storm's path felt the pain of rereading act of God clauses in their insurance forms. In Brooklyn, hurricane day is gray, temperate, and breezy. We can see brief disappointed hopes flare around us with each gust.

Later, I turn on my laptop and can type again. Some of the keys seem to be doing strange things. Eventually, I figure out that the keyboard thinks it's in the Japanese Romaji setting, and I can't fix it. I resign myself to learning how to use a Japanese keyboard. A paranoid part of me wonders if this is some kind of parting blow from the universe for faded sins. The rest of me just thinks something always happens, whether we notice it or not, and we never know what to look for before it passes.

INADEQUATE REMINDERS

Sitting on the train from Philadelphia to Penn Station, I'm still inextricably hung up on a thought that's been with me since I stepped off the train running the other way: how little I remember of my childhood home.

I don't actually have a childhood home the way many people do. I moved too many times, and can't ever answer the question "Where did you grow up?" in less than five minutes and, if possible, a thoughtful swig of beer with which to sort out the list of suburbs, cities, and backwaters I remember dimly, if at all. When asked where I was born, I say San Francisco, because being born took much less time than growing up, and Bell Atlantic didn't have time to transfer my father's job while I was working through it. Since I live on the East Coast, saying I was born in San Francisco always lights the questioner's eyes with the assumption that I'm an alien from a better world with blue waters, state-sponsored dope, and an absence of New Jersey. Their next question always disappoints them, because we moved to Pennsylvania six months later, and I know nothing about San Francisco.

That put me in Wynnewood, Pennsylvania, which is the childhood home I just left. I don't remember that particular tenure at all, beyond a single memory of visiting my grandmother, who was living in our attic at the time. It's not as creepy as it sounds; the attic in that house was bigger and better decorated than my current apartment, and probably would have cost half the price had she been paying for it. She used to feed me brightly colored vitamins, in the hopes of getting me hooked on them. It helped me get hooked on skittles and, later, amphetamines, but the intent was blameless.

After that we moved to Virginia, where I remember having a lot of nightmares. A few years later we came back to Wynnewood, bought the house from my grandmother, kicked her out of the attic, and that's where I lived from five to nine. Since that's longer than I've lived anywhere besides Brooklyn, it's as much a childhood home as I'm going to get.

I'm not a parent, but I imagine five to nine to be one of the more horrifying periods of childhood for a parent to endure. The child is still cruel and stupid, but moderately capable of moving around on their own, and most parents feel obligated to let them explore. So this was the first home where I could take brief trips out into the world without supervision. There were boundaries, of course. Not a well-mapped fence, but a set of check-in times and places, and waypoints where I could be found in case I missed a check-in. But despite these limits, this was a place rich with memories.

Or so I assumed. Turned out there weren't a lot of memories. For a given hot spot, I could summon four or five at most, usually just some vague impressions so old and dim they were hard to distinguish from a dream or total fabrication. Occasionally I'd get a memory of being inside a house, but would have no idea which house. A few memories got fondly remembered for an hour or more, until I realized they were from a visit several years after I'd moved away. After the usual shock of wondering why everything was so goddamn small and close together (since my legs are now twice as long and I lazily stroll twice as fast), I found that many of my memories were geographically impossible, and must be composites made from other, utterly forgotten events.

I had sunk the entire town into wistful recollection, despairing of the possibility of new memories, and the memories I had were few, spotty, and about 50 percent false.

I think people who live in one place prior to college have a more thorough mental catalogue of their past. When I go through old pictures, my first thought about each is wondering where I was living at the time. If you live in one place, new events happen where old events happened, and the place serves as mute witness, carrying forward memories from the time you were here and did this and talked about the last time you were there and did that, and so on.

My memory is events and places, but the places are so varied and distant from one another that the location is just a feature, and might as well be another place that looks kind of like it.

I walked around, trying to trace paths forged twenty years ago. They were very short paths. Here we got some change from our parents, and then we walked over here, and, according to my memory, fell unconscious and woke up eight months later in school. Did we walk farther down the road? No idea. Probably I was at a waypoint, not to go into the great beyond, and had to get back for check-in time. If I ever went past the beaten paths, I didn't go often enough and nothing interesting enough happened to make it into the mental hall of fame.

I walked over a bridge I remembered as completely as any other feature of the town, only to reach the other side in totally unfamiliar territory. I felt a little like Rupert Everett driving out of town at the end of *Cemetery Man* only to find out there's nothing outside the town but a giant cliff, and he has to go back to the insensible neosurrealist life he was trying to flee. I walked on, since it wasn't a movie, and there wasn't a real cliff. I was hoping something in the town would connect another part of the narrative.

This part of town was called Mainline, for whatever reason, and was populated by the upper middle class as a breeding ground for fraternity brothers and practical yet expensive cars. This led to a parade of unironic signs, which, read as imperatives, suggested activities ranging from the uplifting (MAINLINE LIFE) to the hedonistic (MAINLINE SMOOTHIES) to the sadistic (MAINLINE COINS). The coffee shop, having either a more developed sense of humor or none at all, called itself Milkboy. It probably would have been a funky little coffee shop anywhere else, but since it was on the Mainline in Pennsylvania, it was basically Starbucks. That's what I was looking for, so I was happy, except that in this Starbucks-but-not-Starbucks I didn't know the local customs. Was the change too little of a tip? Was I supposed to be happy at them if they weren't happy? Should I reach out my hand for the coffee, or wait for them to put it down? I was an alien here, a stranger who didn't merely read about New York City but lived there, and probably knew as many as six or seven black people.

I'm being a little unfair. But I was not from this town anymore. As I walked around, I didn't remember anything. I must have come here, often, in the back of a practical car, to shop and follow my parents around. But all that was gone. I went to the local bars, and watched the patrons, wondering if I played with any of them in 1988. All the patrons close to my age were too young, and were almost universally crew-cut young Republicans, putting on a little beer weight and wearing a demure stud in whichever ear they thought wouldn't make them gay.

On the way back to my bed at the family friend's house, I knew that I was as far from home as I could get. I crossed the bridge again, and got the now familiar, creeping sensation where my feet knew exactly where to go but I was neither immersed in discovering anew, nor feeling anything familiar and comfortable. Everything was just recognizable enough to be mundane, but never sparked any actual recollection or nostalgia. This town, as a place, was dead to my mind.

My memories while exploring the old turf didn't amount to much more than what I remember when my mind wanders on long bus trips. A lot of formative experiences probably happened there, creating thoughts that led to other thoughts, bouncing down the long corridor of the internal monologue I refer to as I. Whatever I am now that came from my past is an echo from a dead musician's chorus.

Now, typing this up this metamemory, I think some urge to embrace the new is in knowing the past is fading. It's not necessarily bad, but I'm pretty sure it's true.

EULOGY

For reasons of inattentiveness, disinterest, and lack of experience, I assumed pallbearers were hired help until I was asked to be one. In China, pallbearers are volunteers, and it's considered a blessing to be one, though it's still polite to tip. Westerners put it on the friends and family, or you can pay the funeral parlor for extra help.

I sit in the third row, to be available but out of the way. I came for Leah. To the rest I am an acquaintance, if not a stranger: the boyfriend of their daughter, sister, niece, or cousin. I also chose the third row because I left my glasses in the car, and, from this distance, the figure in the casket is a human-shaped blur instead of the remains that might remind me of all the remains I've avoided seeing in my life.

Leah's mother is running around distracted, unable to focus. She's trying to find two more people to help carry the casket. If I'd known what she was looking for, and known the only other guests capable of bearing the weight were me and Leah's sister's boyfriend, I would have offered. I'm trying not to interfere with anyone else's emotions, so I sit quietly and think to myself until she asks me. When Leah first told me her grandmother died, I did the same thing until she asked me to come with her. I want to be there for her, but sometimes being there for someone means shutting up and being somewhere else.

My family has given me a pass on funerals, partly because I'm not close with much of my extended family, partly because I was all but alone in the room when I held my grandfather's hand and told him it was okay to die. So I've only been to two in my whole life. The other was five months ago.

◆

"Did you talk to Ria?" asks Tall Paul. We called him Tall Paul until we discovered Big Paul was taller, so we gave up and called him Asian Paul for a while, and later settled on Ethnic Friend.

"No?" I expected something having to do with the pool team, or a party, or a surprise for one of our friends, or advice, or a story sitting somewhere between gossip and a life lesson, or even a scolding for something I'd done and hadn't yet realized was wrong. These are the kinds of things that I expected when someone told me to talk to Ria.

I find her in the back. She gives me a wide smile and a hug, then puts me in front of her and says, "I have lung cancer."

This is the first time I cry. She gives me another hug.

"I know, and I just quit smoking. Little too late, I guess. It's okay. I'm going to fight it. I'm starting the chemo this week, and I'm gonna beat it."

We talk for a while, and once she's calmed me down, I sit with Tall Paul and other friends, and we relax. We're worried, but none of us actually expect her to die. It's Ria, for fuck's sake. Nothing can beat Ria. Ria's the one who helps all of us. Ria has the energy of ten five-year-olds and a will to live that could raise the dead. This is the woman who can make a dozen strange dogs sit at once, who nursed a pigeon back from a broken wing, who makes more art than an art school, and who I guess ran this bar on the side.

She didn't tell us it was stage IV. That her chances were fifty-fifty of being alive in eight months. Less after that. I guess I'm glad she didn't admit she could leave us.

◆

In the beginning, a pallbearer just bore the pall, the sheet that's laid over the casket, while other, and presumably stronger, men carried the actual casket. Since a sheet is not a difficult thing to carry, it's fitting that the bearer of the pall should take over the rest of the duties: Nowadays, the hearse does most of the grunt work, followed by the cart, which can be guided and steadied by two people. Our actual physical work is moving the casket between the cart and the hearse, and, finally, from the hearse to the grave.

I sit with Leah for a while in a room away from the wake. When I'm not with Leah, I'm keeping my brain busy trying to figure out the logistics of a time-travel novel, and smoking more than usual.

People introduce themselves to me, and ask who I am. "Hi, I'm Peter, Leah's boyfriend." My singular identity gives me anonymity. The conversation rarely goes past the introduction: I think meeting me is a moment when they can talk about something else for a few seconds.

There are eight wreaths, one for each pallbearer to carry. There's a small bench in front of the casket, to kneel on while saying good-bye to the dead. There's a crucifix in the casket, and a picture.

The funeral directors are polite and firm in every direction they give. At first it seems brusque to me, but I realize that they are doing exactly the right thing: being professional and calm and telling people who don't know what to do what to do.

They make a last call of sorts, asking the friends, then the family, to come forward and pay their respects. When the rest have filed out, and only the family and the pallbearers remain, the director and his assistant prepare to close the casket. The director turns a silent crank to lower the woman's head. They tuck her in. The director asks if they would like to take the crucifix and the picture out, or leave them. The family takes the crucifix but leaves the picture. The director stands back and looks over every detail. "That's perfect," he says. "I'm going to close the casket now. There's going to be a little noise when it latches." He informs us of every step.

As the family goes to their cars, I wait with six strangers and the other boyfriend. The director first tells us to each take a wreath to what seems to be the wreath car. Then the casket is wiped down, and we lift it onto a cart. It takes all of us.

On the way out, we pause at the top of the ramp while the hearse is prepared, and I look down at the closed casket, containing the final repose of a woman I never met.

◆

The first chemo treatment didn't work.

Then the second chemo treatment didn't work.

When I reflect on losing someone, I wonder how I'll feel, since it's different each time, and it makes my brain snap. I wonder how many people will feel sorry for me, and for how long. I wonder what sort of behavior I can get away with. Quit my job? Leave the state? If my whole family died, I could do pretty much anything, as long as I left a note. Less for one parent? A friend? The question of what to do after the hypothetical loss forces its way into my mind, blocking the horror of what could be lost before it hits me.

Ria takes a turn for the worse two weeks before she dies. An infection. She seems to recover from it. Most of us still don't believe she's going to die. When I see her in the hospital, she's still laughing between coughs. I realize afterward how shocked and quiet I was, sitting next to her hospital bed.

A few days later, she takes another turn for the worse, and goes to hospice care. The next day at work, I sit through an all-hands meeting for my company. I sit in the back, and for an hour, nothing goes through my head except for the endless repetition of, *I don't give a fuck. I don't give a fuck. I don't give a fuck.*

That night, I write an e-mail to a few coworkers telling them what's going on. I tell them I'll be at the hospital for the next few days, and that there's no need to write back.

I meet Ria's family at the hospital, and her sister's voice nearly starts me crying, because its lilt is the same as Ria's used to be. Ria can now barely speak. I listen to her family speak Dutch as Ria slips in and out of morphine sleep in the next room. I fold origami cranes, because when somebody asked Ria what she wanted, she said a thousand cranes.

In the mornings, I can't stay in bed. When I open and close my eyes, my mind tries to pretend I'm her. She drifts around her medicated consciousness, her heart racing to make up for a lost lung, awake long enough to see a few more of the people coming in and out. A line of hundreds who love her.

She keeps winking at us when we see her. She tries to speak, but we can't make out anything except our names. We can tell she's smiling by the crinkles in her eyes. We file in one and two at a time, to grip her hand and say hello.

We fold cranes for hours in the hospital and at the bar. Hundreds of them. At some point, I realize nobody has told my ex-fiancée, so I tell her, and she comes to visit. While waiting, she folds with us. Abruptly, she says, "I'm folding these because I don't know what else to do." The rest of us look down. There is nothing else to do. I think that's why Ria told us to do it.

Ria sees me standing next to my ex and seems ecstatic, since we were one of the catastrophes Ria tried to haul back from the brink, and she loved seeing us together, not screaming or throwing things at each other. My ex leaves her new children's book for her.

Outside, my ex and I say good-bye. We don't touch, and we don't say anything to hurt each other.

◆

It's beginning to rain when we put the casket into the hearse. We ride in the limo for about a block, and stop in front of the church. In the first hiccup of the day, we're left in the limo for the next ten minutes, waiting for the hearse, and the air conditioner is broken. Even as the least dressed-up person in the car, it gets uncomfortable, and I lead the way out to stand under the half-umbrella of a tree.

The director instructs us that we're supposed to walk next to the casket, each of us with one hand on the pall, as the director's assistant pulls the cart along. I keep my eyes straight ahead, staring at the giant picture of Jesus on the cross painted on the wall. When we get to the front, the family is told to sit in the front right-hand pews, the pallbearers in the left. A couple of the pallbearers go over to comfort their relatives or spouses on the right. I don't want to be disruptive, so I stand there, wondering if I should go over, until the priest starts to speak.

I'm told later that the priest was good and didn't drag it out too much. The extent to which this astounds me is indicative to how little I know of Catholicism. Between the prayers and hymns, I want the guy to shut up a full hour before he actually does. I have to stand sometimes, and all the standing and sitting is so confusing I have to sneak peeks over my shoulder to try to follow the crowd.

The prayers and hymns are mostly dictated by the church, and it immediately angers me that most of it is propaganda for God-fearing. "Saving" and "serving" and "Jesus" pound down on my ears, but I try to ignore them, because it's the ritual, the director, and the tradition that's giving everybody here a place to start. At some point, I think the casket is moving, and I realize I'm about to have an anxiety attack, so I tune out the priest and try to do multiplication in my head. It turns out to be harder than I remember, and I have to write some of it out on my hand. I recall that autism is on a scale, but I know I'm not autistic, and then I realize that I'm writing on the hand that will have to be on the pall on the way out, so I try to rub it off during the next prayer.

Eventually, Leah reads her eulogy. Now I tear up, because I'm watching my girlfriend cry. This is the last official goodbye. The part where you accept that a person no longer is, only was.

◆

As I help Elisabeth fold her second crane, Alex comes to the table, takes my hand, and says, "She's gone."

Elisabeth looks at me, her mouth open. I let go of Alex and pull her to my shoulder as she starts crying. The words are sinking into me, the tingling shock spreading. We clutch each other for a minute, until I pull her up to find others. We go to Tall Paul at the bar. His face is a mask except for the tears streaming down his cheeks. Then I start to sob. I sob until it hurts, then catch my breath and ask nobody, "Where's Diego?" I find Diego in the backyard. I grab his hand across the picnic table and we hold each other until the shaking stops.

I notice a couple sitting behind me during this. They're halfway through their drinks, looking around uncomfortably. I half-laugh, imagining what they'll write on Yelp: "Drinks were fairly priced, lot of crane decorations. Atmosphere was good until twenty grown men burst into tears all at once. Bar didn't look Irish, not sure if that happens a lot." Then another sob hits me and I can't breathe.

The next day, at the crawfish cookout that we'd hoped Ria might see, people come in unrested, some somber, some antsy. It speaks to our closeness that what would usually go unspoken is spoken. If everyone waited until their tears were spent, nobody would come back for months, so there are bursts of silence and turning heads. There's a note from Ria somewhere that people keep telling me to read, but I can't find it.

Everybody feels on their own schedule, moving to find each other, moving to be alone, stepping into the bathroom and locking it for a few minutes.

"Ten-minute distractions," says Tim, choking up as we share a cigarette. "Ten-minute distractions."

◆

We set the casket holding Leah's grandmother above the grave, then stand next to it, across from the family. We all talked through the ride here. At the end of the ceremony, leading up to this moment, it seems to get a little harder. Everyone has walked the prescribed paces to one last moment.

There's more speaking. When it's done, everybody walks by and throws a flower beside the grave. The pallbearers are instructed to throw theirs last, then walk away. We're done. The family says good-bye.

We all head back to the cars. Leah is still tearing up, but less now.

Everybody seems relieved, still quietly sad, but ready to deal with the next thing, and maybe the thing after that. I see the emptiness I don't share; here, I'm only assisting in the ritual of beginning to fill it.

◆

When people in the bar business die, the funerals are not small.

There are hundreds of us. I'm surprised by how many I recognize, surprised even more by how many I consider friends. For the first time, I realize the extent of the family that collected around Ria in her life, and how careful she was in attracting the best and kindest parts of the world around her. There is no wake, no open casket, and there are no speeches by anyone not close to Ria. We drive the cars close to the grave, then walk to where the plain wooden box is suspended above it. We are an ocean of black on the grass, beneath a blue sky.

Harold reads his eulogy. When he says *sun,* the sun breaks out from the clouds. When he says *breeze,* the wind picks up.

And then, because Ria would have the last word at her own funeral, her sister reads her note:

> Ah . . . I wanted to write poems about my
> parting. I wanted to write you all individual
> notes and letters, but it appears now that I
> may run out of time again. Lately that seems
> to be the case. I asked for a couple of months
> at least. Well that was not happening. Then I
> said all I need is a couple of good weeks. A
> couple of weeks they gave, just not the good
> part I asked for. And now they cannot prom-

ise me a week. Ha! So I'll have to skip the po-
ems, consolidate the notes and letters, and get
straight to the point.

To all my dear friends. I have thoroughly en-
joyed sharing my life with you. The laughs,
the tears, the fun, the fights, the ups and
downs. You've made my life colorful! Each of
you being so different from each other. I truly
appreciate all of you. And I will continue doing so from the other side.

P.S. If I've ever hurt you, know that it was
never on purpose and I apologize. And if I put
a smile on your face, know that it was my
pleasure.

I love you.

Ria

Leaving, I hug Diego and Holden for far too long. It's not
a moment we want to keep, but we want to stop any more
time from passing.

Sunday, the butterflies come. They seem to think they own the sidewalks, and are annoyed to have to flutter over our shoulders as they fly to food and friends. In that respect, there is nothing unusual about them as butterflies or New Yorkers, but a butterfly by the BQE in Brooklyn is usually something worth pointing out, not something you have to wave out of your face every two minutes.

◆

When an Italian grandmother dies, there is food. I know from Leah's eulogy that food and love were woven close in her grandmother's heart, and the gathering is almost festive, once the wine sinks in.

We're sitting at the kids' table, or the everyone-between-thirty-and-forty table. Everybody seems okay, but I try not to get too drunk because I know the kind of thoughts that seeming okay can be covering. I fail, because I'm trying to be there for Leah and not think about Ria, and proper numbing is the only way to accomplish that. I end up having a protracted conversation with Leah's cousin, trying to help her figure out how to get a date. The demands are extensive: Over six feet, enough money to raise a family, emotionally available, and not a dick. I tell her she's too short to make under six feet a deal breaker. She says I may be right but she's still shooting for it.

Another cousin wants to make a speech, but never finds the moment.

We get back to Leah's parents' home, and I think we're going back to the city, but there's a dinner to be had, so I pass out on a chair until Leah puts me to bed. Later, she wakes me up and we go to a teppanyaki restaurant. They don't have a liquor license, so I bring in the bottle of Jameson Leah and I picked up the night before, and convince her brother to take a shot out of a sauce bowl. Later, the cook squirts sake from a ketchup bottle into the mouth of anyone who can catch a bit of avocado he tosses off his knife. I catch the avocado easily, but wait too long with the sake, and end up spraying a couple of shots' worth on my plate. It's the most fun I've had at a restaurant in years.

On the train home, Leah and I all but sleep, spent from the day.

◆

2012 was a year of death for me and mine. So much so that half of us are still wondering who's next. It started before Ria, and it's still happening. I once said aloud, "Fuck it. I hope the world does end in December." I say life is a fight we cannot win, and the point is the fight. This fight is getting too hard and confusing, but even when I can't do it anymore, I just take the next step, and do the next thing, and wait for instruction. A little Turing machine flipping bits to keep itself alive.

I don't understand what happens to the brain when it grieves. Thoughts you'd think belong to other emotions spring to mind, stripped of context, and they feel like madness. Sex and rage and fear and selfishness attack with equal ferocity. Explanations and excuses compete to explain and excuse the inexplicable and inexcusable. Sense and reason give way in the face of ultimate loss. The human being is a motion between other human beings, and when one is gone, there's no movement that can get it back.

Some days I wake up and it doesn't seem real. Realizations come in as if slowly translated from a foreign language. Ria will never play pool again. Ria will never come to a party again. Ria will never kiss me good-bye again. Ria will never laugh again. Ria won't stop by. Ria is gone. One by one, I remove expectations and routines, trying to close up or fill the holes so I won't stumble in them tomorrow.

I like living with cats because I can blame them for all the noises in the night. Now I want those noises to be Ria's ghost. I don't believe in ghosts, but I'll spend the next four years talking to the reflection of her she built in my thoughts. Sometimes it will feel real enough, which is a tribute to her, and perhaps schizophrenia.

The dead don't care what we do, because there's no they anymore. Mourning their deaths and celebrating their lives, through whatever means, is how the living find ways to go on. Stripped of tradition and superstition, I have found other rituals. I go to the bar. I cry. I speak to my friends. I work. I get coffee at Starbucks every day at three. I eat my lunch alone, with a book and a glass of wine. They are the same rituals I always follow. They are rituals of life, but serve well as rituals of death. I practice them because they are my map of what to do when there's nothing to do, and there's no place to begin not doing it.

FULL DISCLOSURE: DEALING

I try to be honest with my doctors about my various mental issues, which means I have to refuse psychoactive medication once or twice a year. Since I'm functional, employed, and happy about 80 percent of the time, I don't want to risk upsetting the delicate stalemate of existing problems, troublesome as they are. I also expect they would medicate the root of all these problems, which is the hyperactive hypothesis machine in my head that I can't turn off. There are a host of tiring aphorisms about how we define ourselves by our struggles or pains or losses or whatever; I call bullshit. We define ourselves by how we think, and if we can feed ourselves, who cares how many people think our thinking is broken? It gets the job done.

So when I tell people not to worry about this or that, or stop being paranoid, or to please, please stop reading their horoscopes as if stars that may not even exist anymore gave a shit, I'm doing it from the perspective of having a whole lot of nonsense rattling around in my head. I'm roughly the same brain as the person who feng shuis the mother-chi out of their apartment and collects feathers for spiritual strength and cleans their aura every Tuesday because Tuesday is a good aura-cleaning day. I have the same thoughts that lead people to think Satan is whispering in their ear and the only way to escape Hell is to kowtow to a dead carpenter for their entire lives. I've made the same rambling and random connections as the person who thinks the CIA is bugging their house because they've found the missing links in JFK's assassination and it's all because of Area 51.

Everybody has that brain. It's a matter of severity and attitude. My level of severity has been high enough to cause people to suggest I should be medicated, but not high enough to prevent me from functioning most of the time. The thing that has caused people to consider me rational for most of my life is that I was fortunate enough to grow up around people who responded to my inquiries with, "Yeah, the brain does a lot of random shit, you'll be fine," or at least, "Shut up and do the dishes." I managed to grow up with no superstitions because I didn't give credence to the part of my head that's drooling on itself and screaming for reasons and connections and stories. I was encouraged to look outward more often than inward, because there's a lot of new things out there to distract from the irrational noise produced by the amygdala. Not all doctors would diagnose me with a nameable problem: People who think the most important thing for me is to be personable and profitable would immediately pump me full of pills, while people who investigate what I actually want and how that affects other people generally let me off the hook.

Diagnostic terms are thrown around loosely in modern parlance, and as a result people can use them to label their thought static as something inherently bad and beat themselves up about it or use it as an excuse. If you can maintain a consistently coherent dialogue with a handful of people, you're okay, and the occasional undeniable knowledge that there's a skeleton under the deck who will grab your ankles if you don't leap over the stairs is not a sign of actual madness, it's just that rationality is something we managed to patch onto the human condition with a lot of trial and error over the last few thousand years, and doesn't ship with the brain we get coming out of the womb. Nobody is rational in the ideal sense of the word. Everybody's doing the best they can to get what they want with the meat sacks they have.

OBSERVATIONS OF A STRAIGHT WHITE MALE WITH NO INTERESTING FETISHES

I was at an erotic fiction reading when I realized I was a fraud. It wasn't that I didn't like the reading. It wasn't that I couldn't relate. It was how I related. As I stood in my ironically faux-leather women's jacket and sipped my overpriced wine, my mind's eye jumped out and turned to see a dilettante searching for the finer points of titillation, among people on the well-lubed edge of redefining sexual identity. My sexual identity is only slightly more complicated than tic-tac-toe. What was I doing? How did I get this far, and how had I not been found out?

In this moment, I decided to figure out how I'd gotten there and what good it would do for me to stick around, because I very much wanted to stay.

I consider myself lucky not to have any obsessions that would have limited my sex life later. My first exposure to the sexualized female form was a *Playboy,* yet I've never been aroused by an airbrush, and after the initial shock of finding out what women really looked like, I was relieved to find their skin wasn't laminated, and I wasn't going to have my skull crushed between a pair of concrete breasts. Lacking real porn, but having family friends who helped develop the consumer Internet, I'm proud to say I'm among the first few hundred people to type the word *smut* into a search engine. Later, in the mid-nineties, long before the Internet became a cornucopia of video porn, I discovered erotic fiction, to which I credit my thorough knowledge of the Latin terms I needed to look things up in *The Joy of Sex,* a book which should be burned both for subtextual homophobia and so we can stop the hippies from mating.

My fascination with erotic fiction put me at risk for getting a hard-on from seeing five to twenty pages of stapled printer paper, which could have been hell in college, but it geared up an imagination that I could effectively apply to the Swimsuit Issue and, between Februaries, Marvel comics. Considering how long it took me to get my hands on real porn, I'm still surprised I never developed a superhero fetish and spent the rest of my life at comic conventions.

I went to a great college for sex: an isolated liberal arts affair where sex was just what you did on the rare occasions you couldn't find drugs. You only had to be slightly more confident or good-looking than I was to be running from orgy to orgy with dozens of stunning strangers. Sadly, you did have to be slightly more good-looking or confident than I was. Not getting laid at all while listening to most of my peers bang headboards probably contributed to the strangest sexual experience I ever had: losing my sex drive altogether, at seventeen. For about a month I became asexual, and was very confused about it. Even more curious, my lust switched back on while standing in line at Walmart looking at a picture of Kevin Sorbo on a *TV Guide* cover during the height of his career on *Hercules*. I did some testing over the next couple of days and found myself turned on by basically everyone, so I concluded that I was either bisexual, or just really needed to have sex.

It turned out to be the latter, and later in life the episode ceased to surprise me. Men, barring the handful of outliers, are obsessed with sex. A woman who wants to have sex but hasn't for a year is nowhere near as deranged as a man in the same position. The mind of a man undergoes psychotic compensatory readjustments to cope. It's not an accident that violently homophobic men violently rape one another in prison. Many girls I know cite male friends who haven't had sex in a while and claim they're not horny all the time. I've met these friends, and they're wound as tightly as anyone I know, increasingly unable to project the calm they need to attract a mate, and concocting more and more elaborate explanations for their inability to do so. I know this because I've been there, and have no doubt I'll be there again someday. The driving goal for men is to have sex; if that's not going to happen, the driving goal becomes getting stoned, which is the only known treatment for sexual frustration. So it doesn't surprise me that after creating some asexual delusion in my hypersexual mind, my brain was grasping at any form of sexuality it could find.

A few months after my libido rebooted, I managed to find a nice goth girl. Two years of vanilla but engrossing sex later,

I was heartbroken and single, and worse, back in small-town Maine, where there were very few eligible women, with a fixation on goth girls, of which there were five. I had a party with a bunch of old friends and slept with the first girl who seemed both stable and willing.

This is where things started to get weird.

She asked me to hit her. Not lightly. Not a slap. She asked me to punch her in the face, hard. Later she told me her primary fantasy was to be gang raped. I couldn't bring myself to hit her or organize a gang rape, and the continued requests put such a damper on our sex life that I stopped being able to get it up. This ended at another party with her drunkenly telling everyone this little detail, and that was that, but it was a glimpse of a world I knew about but didn't really believe existed.

I didn't investigate at the time, but the experience made the usual sex talk in mid-state Maine so banal I didn't even bother contributing. That plus unmotivated social defaulting landed me in the more interesting sexual circles. In every place that wasn't an isolated art school, that was whatever the local LGBTQBDSMNAACPSMSLOL club was. I was never a member, I just knew everybody. My accidental arrivals to this the scene generally suited me, because elsewhere in Maine you usually had to beat someone up, shoot an animal, or scream a lot to get laid. None of these things came naturally to me. Watching black and white movies, tentacle porn, and waxing bohemian fugue while blackout drunk did come naturally, so my destination was always clear, if not my purpose.

After college, my pseudoalternative lifestyle finally landed me in a fetish bar, watching a bearded octogenarian whip Errol Flynn. He wasn't really Errol Flynn, but I desperately wanted to shout, "Do what you will, sheriff, I'll never talk!"

That urge gave me the first inkling that I was not supposed to be there.

I eventually got into the blood and hot wax and cold water, right around when my gothic wardrobe started to fade into Goodwill bins. I love sensation, which is why I switch the water temperature in the shower from Unitarian heat to Calvinist cold and back, and I'm an avid contributor to the book of interesting things to do with chocolate and wine. But for me, it's all icing for the sensory desserts of life that almost make up for its inevitable punch line. Bondage and pain and not-quite-sex-but-probably-related-to-sex as sciences unto themselves are foreign to me.

The chasm between what I know or see and what I do was made apparent when dominatrix friend of mine sent me a list of services she offers. It goes like this: Corporal punishment, spanking, paddling, caning, flogging, asphyxiation/smothering/breath play, smoking and human ashtray, boot/shoe/foot/leg worship, sensuous torments, verbal humiliation and abuse, physical domination, smacking, spitting, nipple torture, clamps and weights, role-play, teasing and denial, trampling, tickling, cross-dressing/sissification, edge play, interrogation/kidnap/blackmail scenarios, medical, face slapping and spitting, nail fetish, torture, wax play, fire play, electrical play, financial slavery, leather and latex fetish, pup-

py/pony training, bondage, leather, ropes, bandage, stretch
wrap, mummification, abandonment, traditional slave training, couple (d/s) training, group session, and, last but not
least, infantilism. I've done maybe three, and they're the ones
everybody does. I've seen most of them, and know what all of
them are, except for a couple where I made the same educated
guesses you did. I have been a voyeur with no interest in vo-
yeurism, more anthropologist than contributing witness.

Still, I stayed in the scene, getting by on a vague and possibly hallucinatory resemblance to David Bowie, always asking myself, do I belong here? Or am I just Woody Allen with
a riding crop?

The problem is I'm a purist. I like my pizza untopped and
my coffee unseasoned. I don't want to be whipped, suffocat-
ed, humiliated, or forced to question my sexual mores. I don't
have any sexual desires you can't find in between a Girls
Gone Wild video and an issue of *Cheri*. I dread the day a girl
asks me for anal, because I find the sensation subpar and the
cleanup a hassle. I'm much kinkier than the average Catholic
would like, but don't really push the boundaries. Worse, I
can't really distinguish between the more refined sexual titillation and actual sex. I don't get much out of watching people
have sex, and strip clubs are wasted on me. Some people can
take the basics and extrapolate complex sexual play in which
not a single protrusion penetrates an orifice. A friend of mine
once described spending an afternoon with one of her friends
throwing popcorn at a girl and calling her a slut while the girl
tried to get herself off. The same friend told me she was going

out of her mind because she hadn't had sex in a year and a half. For her, this apparently made sense; for me, it was a logical paradox that kept me up, for various reasons, for the rest of the night. On a related, but more orgasmic note, an entirely gay friend of mine slept with two lesbians on the condition that they could fuck him with a strap-on the next day. When I asked him about this, he waved it off and said, "Sex has nothing to do with my sexuality," which makes me scratch my head even now.

I'm not just a little straight: You could hang pictures with my sexual orientation. As a result, I have no homophobia at all; I've made out with more guys than most girls I know, to everyone's frustration. Even that was calculated: If I made out with enough of the guys I could prove my sexual adventurousness, and I'd be allowed to make out with the lesbians when the party started winding down.

I emphatically do not identify as queer. I don't like groups or identities in general, so I never cared about the old gender roles, but creating new labels to skirt old labels always bothers me. I hope this is just a step, since the word *queer* needed to be taken back from the people who used it as a slur in the first place. But the necessity of the step speaks to the sad nature of the debate.

What really buggers my goat is that the word *queer*—in an attempt to cover the myriad and totally unrelated sexual preferences that aren't a man and a woman procreating in the missionary position within sacred matrimony—is often defined as nonheteronormative or, better, outside the normal sexual identities, and breaking the rules of sex and gender. I hate being categorized for things I don't do, and I'm not sure why anybody would cling to a label that took a whole collection of interesting individual identities and lumped them into a negative space defined as not a group of people that are assumed to have no interesting sexual predilections. Using reverse marginalization to polarize the issue, besides leaving people like me out in no-man's-land, is the opposite of nurturing acceptance and tearing down gender assumptions: It gives people who disagree with you a target, and a convenient one, because now they don't have to try to figure out the difference between the lifestyles they might be willing to accept and the ones that are just too weird for them. It turns people not like you into a necessary enemy with which to define yourself. In my life, I've gone from the always-welcome token straight boy to the unenlightened serial monogamist, and now I've discovered I'm the antienlightening white cisgendered heteronormative element in society. The word *heteronormative* was not just incidentally used in place of *heteronormal,* either; *normal* means I'm just white bread on the shelf, while *normative* carries the implication that I'm the stock boy throwing out the rye and the sourdough. This offensive dismissal of my thoroughly contemplated personal sexuality tempts me to suggest another definition for queer, namely, "Doing things Nazis don't like even when white gentiles do them." Overabstracted social clubs are the reason we hear politicians denouncing the acts of foes and praising the identical actions of friends in the same breath. When people start from their symbol for something good and work their way down, individual actions are forever severed at the top, and the similarities of thought and deed that might have drawn out a measure of empathy are lost to the fanatic rabble's need to fight.

You should do what you want and fuck whom you want without having to come up with a name for it. For ease of reproduction, certain organs get roughly equal distribution, and for the sake of sports statistics, we have various levels of testosterone and estrogen, and that's the end of it for me. Convincing people there are scales of gender and preference or that there are poles of open-mindedness that require new terminology seems to me like a waste of time that could be better spent having sex. What if we could backtrack a bit? Imagine what would happen if all across the country, homosexual men stood up and said, "Wait, what are gay and queer? I don't know what you're talking about. I just happen to have a penis and I like fucking men. In fact, my sex life has 50 percent more in common with yours and your spouse's than they do with each other." Getting this label-free dialogue into everyday discourse might be the first step in helping the most tragic victims of any ideological war: the people caught on the wrong side when the camps start digging trenches.

Of course I blame the Christian right for basically everything, but in my principles, I can't see the justification for counterattacking idiots, and I think it's bad form to validate an argument by codifying it on new terms, regardless of whichever side currently owns the terminology. I constantly want to yell at the progressives for not ignoring the philosophical arguments of the aforementioned idiots. Then again, pointlessly raised voices are exactly what I'm arguing against. This puts me in the odd position of not knowing whether or not I'm a hypocrite when I'm at parties with women undressing one another, where I just keep my mouth shut and thank God that Jesus doesn't love me.

Despite my self-righteous haranguing of self-righteousness, the fact remains I'm quietly leeching off a culture that's taking important risks in politics, culture, and pleasure. Since I'm apolitical and a culture of one, I'm not interested in any of the emotional or intellectual aspects of the scene that aren't directly related to ejaculation. For years this protected me from the more common traps that hinder the pursuit of free love. Foremost, I always knew that love isn't free. Intimacy is about being vulnerable, and trusting the people to whom you make yourself vulnerable, and you have to be careful about that because everybody has different ideas about what's safe and acceptable. The whole game is dangerous and complicated and you don't need to be betrayed to get hurt. Nothing is ever completely on the table. I don't think this is bad. Love shouldn't be free. Part of love is sacrifice, not because love needs to hurt, but because things are worth more if you sacrifice for them.

I used to use this as an argument for monogamy, and the square community loves this idea. But this is a myopic view of sacrifice and emotional commitment. The most fanatically monogamous people fallaciously marry the concept of commitment and sacrifice to possessiveness. Possessiveness is strongly encouraged in our society, and in most societies, since our media is under the thumb of drama-industry bigwigs. But when you think about it, possessiveness has nothing to do with love. You can't be vulnerable in front of someone you own. The terms of your commitment are a tentative agreement between you and your beloved, and those terms should be entirely up to the two of you.

The best thing the pursuit of sexual adventure can teach us is how to dissolve the bonds between pleasure, love, possession, and jealousy. People on both ends of the sexual spectrum of experimentation have preached to me that sex with love is the best; I don't think that's true. I've had plenty of mediocre sex with people I loved, and I've had explosive, mind-blowing sex with people I refer to as "French girl" and "I think it started with a T." Physical pleasure, love, and fidelity are not the same thing. Even if your requirements for intimacy make them inextricable, confusing them has been the beginning of many dramas, and none of them were necessary.

When I was not exactly monogamous, an astute friend of mine said I wasn't really polyamorous. This is true, partly because I don't want my sex life encoded. I don't have a unique set of terms to apply to my shenanigans. I also don't have a backup girl, or fuck buddies, or a BFF. Each relationship with a person in my life is a relationship between me and that person, neither representative of an abstract belief nor fundamentally dependent on a relationship with a third party. I wasn't waiting for the person I'm going to be monogamous with, nor was I trying to build a harem. I still don't have a name for what I want or what I do. I don't have a group that defines me, nor do I want to belong to one. I don't think anybody should. I think the political division of human sexuality is abhorrent, regardless of who started it, but despite all the grumbling and grating edges between gay, straight, queer, intersex, hetero, homo, bi, trans, top, bottom, up, down, strange, and charmed, there's a rhapsody of voices calling for the acceptance and exploration of our kaleidoscopic libidos, and it pushes us ever closer to the point where we realize we cannot even pretend to tame or avoid the chaos of sex and love, and where we must accept the individuality and uniqueness of every relationship and each desire. To anyone who would claim that that's too complicated and hard for people to grasp without neat categories, I say we should start getting used to it, because that's the way it is, and denying it only creates frustration and misunderstanding.

DATING 101: THE RIGHT AMOUNT OF SKY

I woke up on the day of the date young, unemployed, and in New York. I don't remember her name, or how we met, or what we talked about. My unemployment probably explains why we went for a walk by the river instead of to a bar.

The lack of detail in my memory of her would have troubled me then, when a date wasn't a common thing in my life. Even though I'm sure I didn't find her attractive, I remember an indistinct charm, and any connection to another human being in the early days must have been sweet, and needed. The hundreds of dates I would go on and thousands of people I would meet afterward made sorting out memories a chaotic process as the years went by. Statistically, she was most likely a brunette between five-foot-two and five-foot-eight. Other than that, I honestly can't even remember if it was really a date. I only remember it at all because of where she took me, and how I got home.

She took me to a walkway somewhere in southwestish Brooklyn that looked out at southern Manhattan across the East River.

Growing up in the country and in flat, sprawling suburbs gave me two experiences of seeing space. In the suburbs, you don't. It's just house, house, yard, small park, road, house. There's no real sense of a landscape outside a mental map.

The country is the opposite: everything is horizons, distant edges, hills and mountains. I always longed to be in the middle of the distant beauty, even though a moment of reflection brought the realization that I was already on someplace's horizon, and the one that was far away from me probably wasn't much different from where I already was.

The view of the city at night from where we sat cut through a youth's worth of that existential wistfulness. The otherness of the view dropped away. The lights of the buildings reached to just under where the moon might have been in an ancient cosmology, and looked as if the otherwise invisible stars had been yanked out of the sky and stacked for my pleasure. The horizon was pulled forward, and it felt like I could see it and be it at once; it was near and far and old and new, inviting and imposing and filling my sensation of reality.

When my date and I parted, I realized I had no idea where I was or how to get to a subway. This was before the days of smartphones, and the phone I had was dead anyway.

Everybody's had the experience of waiting for a cab in a low traffic area, and eventually giving up and walking to another intersection only to glance back and see a cab going by the spot they just left. However, I believe I belong to a fairly exclusive club of people who can claim this happened to them six times in two hours.

I'm not sure how far I staggered, but it was 3:00 a.m. when a livery driver took pity on me and accepted my twelve dollars in payment for the thirty-dollar trip back to my apartment. Half-conscious, I watched the buildings slide by on our way back north, and for the first time pieced together a few of the disparate destinations I only knew in relation to their subway stops. I felt a bit like a child, looking up at lights on the highway from under the edge of the window, barely knowing or caring what they were. I only knew I wanted more, and might stay a while.